Essential Tropical Fish
Species Guide

Anne Finlay

Elluminet Press
www.elluminetpress.com

Essential Tropical Fish: Species Guide

Publisher: Elluminet Press
Director: Kevin Wilson
Lead Editor: Mike Smith
Copy Editors: Joanne Taylor
Proof Reader: Robert Price
Indexer: James Marsh
Cover Designer: Kevin Wilson

eBook versions and licenses are also available for most titles. Any source code or other supplementary materials referenced by the author in this text is available to readers at

www.elluminetpress.com/resources

For detailed information about how to locate your book's source code, go to

www.elluminetpress.com/resources

Table of Contents

About the Author

Anne Finlay has had a life long fascination with tropical fish from an early age, starting off with keeping gold fish then moving on to tropical and marine fish.

This led to studying them further at college and working at a public aquarium maintaining the tanks and advising people on the various species.

Her experience of the hobby and the fish trade keeps her abreast of the latest developments and has become the basis for writing this book.

Fish are fascinating to watch and hope you enjoy them as much as we have.

Acknowledgements

Thanks to all the staff at Luminescent Media & Elluminet Press for their passion, dedication and hard work in the preparation and production of this book.

To all my friends and family for their continued support and encouragement in all my writing projects.

Introduction

Throughout this book, each fish is categorized according to its temperament and difficulty of care or care level. This should hopefully help you when selecting fish for your tank.

This book contains the most common species found in most aquatic stores and is by no means exhaustive. A lot of species of the same family are very similar, they just have different markings so their needs and requirements are the same. If a particular fish is not in the book, look for a similar species.

First things to take into consideration are, the fish's adult size, its temperament, compatibility with other tank-mates, and care difficulty. These are indicated in the book.

Temperament

Peaceful: Species within this category do not pose a real threat toward other fish, and are very passive and sometimes reclusive in nature.

Semi-Aggressive: Species within this category are normally active fish, and may occasionally chase or show aggression towards one another or similar shaped tank mates.

When placing Semi-Aggressive species in your aquarium, be sure to introduce them after the smaller, more passive fish have been established.

Aggressive: Species within this category are normally territorial and bold fish that should be housed with fish that are of the same demeanour.

Aggressive fish should be housed in a species only aquarium, and if you're adding them to displays with semi-aggressive tank mates, they should be the last fish introduced into the display.

Care Difficulty

Easy: The fish in this category are not too demanding in the care that they require.

Most of these fish do not have any special feeding requirements and can tolerate a wide range of water conditions.

Moderate: Fish in this category demand a bit more care and attention. Some of these fish may have special feeding, lighting parameters and may require water conditions closer to those found in their natural habitat.

Difficult: Fish in this category demand a higher level care and attention with pristine water quality. Many of these fish have special feeding, water and lighting requirements.

They should only be added to an aquarium that is well established and running for many months. These species should be among the last additions to your collection.

Water Parameters

One of the easiest ways to keep your fish healthy is to maintain their ideal water conditions.

Make sure your aquarium has the correct water parameters and environmental requirements for the particular species you are interested in keeping. We have included some general water parameters for each species covered in this book. You can test these parameters using a test kit, which is readily available in most pet stores that stock fish.

While most aquarium species can tolerate a broad range of water conditions, keep in mind that certain delicate species of fish have very specific water parameter requirements.

Temperature

The water temperature of your aquarium plays a vital role in the health of your fish. In the diagram below is what is known as the 'safe zone' for tropical fish and is usually between 25°C & 31°C for most species.

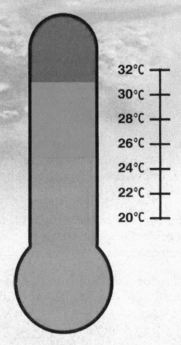

Fish are cold blooded and are very sensitive to temperature changes and any sudden temperature change can wreak havoc on your fish. Invest in a reliable heater to maintain stable water temperature.

Water Hardness (KH)

Carbonate hardness is the measure of carbonate and bicarbonate concentration in your aquarium water and is the main buffering capacity of the water; the ability of the water to resist pH shifts. If there is a high KH then the pH of the water will be stable.

°Degrees of Hardness	Description
0-6	Soft Water
6-12	Moderately Hard
12-20	Hard Water
20-30	Very Hard Water

pH

The pH is the measurement of relative alkalinity or acidity of the water.

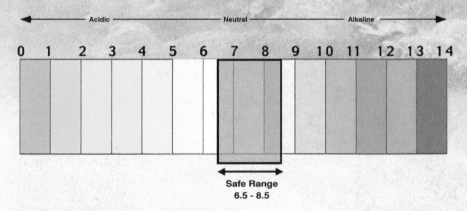

A pH reading of 7.0 is considered neutral.

Lower than 7.0 (down to 0) is acidic.

Higher than 7.0 (up to 14) is alkaline.

Livebearers

As the name suggests, these fish give birth to live young instead of laying eggs.

Poeciliidae, commonly known as livebearers, are all very hardy and are considered to be a good fish for beginners, are a lot of fun and many experienced fish keepers continue to delight in keeping them!

Because these fish bare live young, they can breed quite rapidly. So keep this in mind if you mix males and females. It is recommended that males and females are not mixed as they will breed and males will relentlessly hassle females.

There are lots of different varieties with lots of different colours readily available.

They tend to inhabit the top and middle of the aquarium but go down to the bottom now and again.

Platy

Palties have various markings and colours, some are red, black, blue, tuxedo - red and back and so on, but are generally the same shape and size.

Scientific Name: Xiphophorus Maculatus
Care Level: Easy
Temperament: Peaceful
Maximum Size: 3" (7.5cm)
Minimum Tank Size: 10 Gallons (40 litre)
Water Conditions: 64-78° F, 17-25° C, KH 10-25, pH 7.0-8.2
Diet: Omnivore – offer them a good quality flake food
Origin: North and Central America
Aquarium Type: Community

Notes:
The Platy requires an aquarium of at least 10 gallons that is densely planted with hardy plants like java fern and java moss.

The Platy is a very peaceful fish and is compatible with most other peaceful fish and is best to keep them in groups of 3 or more. Don't mix with aggressive species.

Platies are omnivores and will eat any prepared flaked and algae based foods.

Guppy

Guppies come in all different colours and look spectacular in a group of 6 or more. Males are generally more colourful that females, but the females are larger.

Scientific Name: Poecilia Reticulata
Care Level: Easy
Temperament: Peaceful
Maximum Size: 2" (5cm)
Minimum Tank Size: 10 Gallons (40 litre)
Water Conditions: 64-82° F, 17-27° C, KH 10-30, pH 5.5-8.4
Diet: Omnivore – offer then a good quality flake food
Origin: South America, Caribbean
Aquarium Type: Community

Notes:
They are hardy and playful and are great beginner fish. They love planted tanks with plenty of space to swim around. They breed very quickly so care should be taken when mixing males and females an all male tank is usually recommended.

Feed them with both algae-based foods as well as meaty foods. An algae-based flake food, along with freeze-dried bloodworms, tubifex, and brine shrimp will provide guppies with the proper nutrition.

They seem to be compatible with most other peaceful fish but beware of fin nippers such as barbs and tetras as they can't resist nipping the guppy's large tail fins.

Endler's Livebearer

These fish are very similar to guppies, although they are smaller and look quite spectacular in large groups of about 12 or more. Some have different markings but are usually the same shape and size.

Scientific Name: Poecilia Wingei
Care Level: Easy
Temperament: Peaceful
Maximum Size: 1" (2.5cm)
Minimum Tank Size: 20 Gallon (75 litre)
Water Conditions: 64-82° F, 17-25° C, KH 10-30, pH 5.5-8.0
Diet: Omnivore
Origin: Venezuela
Aquarium Type: Community

Notes:
Keep in a group of at least 6 or more but watch out for fin nipping fish such as barbs or tetras as they will rip the guppies tail to shreds.

Plants should be hardy varieties such as java fern and java moss that can handle the increased hardness in the aquarium. Other peaceful fish would make good tank mates.

These fish are omnivore and require both algae-based foods as well as meaty foods. An algae-based flake food will be fine

Molly

Mollies are cheeky and alert and can be trained to come up to the glass when they see you and even hand fed with a bit of patience. They have various different markings but generally look similar in shape and size.

Scientific Name: Poecilia Latipinna
Care Level: Easy
Temperament: Peaceful
Maximum Size: 4" – 5" (10cm)
Minimum Tank Size: 20 Gallons (75 litre)
Water Conditions: 75-82° F, 23-27° C, KH 10-25, pH 7.5-8.5
Diet: Omnivore – offer a good quality flake food
Origin: Central America
Aquarium Type: Community

Notes:
Give them a tank of at least 20 gallons, densely planted with plenty of strong plants such as java fern, sagittaria, vallisneria and anubias.

They require a good filtration system because of their hearty appetites and will pretty much eat anything. Offer them an algae-based flake food, as well as freeze-dried bloodworms, tubifex, and brine shrimp. They love it.

Mollies seem to be compatible with most other peaceful fish and is best to keep 3 or more.

Sword Tail

Sword tails can be identified with their sword like tail fin. They have various markings and colours but are generally the same shape and size.

Scientific Name: Xiphophorus Hellerii
Care Level: Easy
Temperament: Peaceful
Maximum Size: 4" (10cm)
Minimum Tank Size: 20 Gallons (75 litre)
Water Conditions: 64-82° F, 17-25° C, KH 12-30, pH 7.0-8.3
Diet: Omnivore - offer them a good quality flake food
Origin: Central America & China
Aquarium Type: Community

Notes:
These guys require an aquarium of at least 20 gallons that is well planted with plenty of room for swimming. Also provide plenty of shelter.

Swordtails are omnivore and will eat flaked foods as well as freeze dried bloodworms, tubifex and brine shrimp.

Swordtails seem to be compatible with most other peaceful fish and are best kept in groups of 3 or more.

Loaches

Loaches belong to the Cobitidae family and are active bottom dwelling scavengers ideally suited for the community aquarium.

Loaches are some of the most popular of all tropical fish, adding colour, interest, and beauty to any larger community aquarium.

Some loaches can get very big so keep this in mind when purchasing.

Loaches are social creatures and must be kept in groups of six or more to minimize aggression and should not be kept alone.

Bengal Loach

Also known as the geto or queen loach, these loaches are easily identified by their stripes and spots.

Scientific Name: Botia Dario
Care Level: Easy
Temperament: Peaceful – bottom dweller
Maximum Size: 6" (15cm)
Minimum Tank Size: 70 Gallon (250 litre)
Water Conditions: 72-86° F, 22-30° C, KH 8-12, pH 6.0-7.5
Diet: carnivorous – offer a good quality sinking pellet food
Origin: Bangladesh and India.
Aquarium Type: Community

Notes:
These loaches should be kept in groups of 5 or more due to their social nature.

They are usually peaceful with other fish, but there have been reports of some feisty specimens. However, any aggression is directed towards each other. This loach seems to be compatible with most other fish species, with the exception of long-finned fish.

The substrate should consist of fine sand in order to protect the delicate sensory barbel area, and plenty of hiding places should be provided rocky caves and robust aquatic plants. The lighting should be subdued.

Big Blue Botia

This fish is very similar to the clown loach but is a bit more aggressive towards each other.

Scientific Name: Yasuhikotakia Modesta
Care Level: Moderate
Temperament: Can be highly territorial, a lot of in-fighting will be seen
Maximum Size: 10"-12" (30cm)
Minimum Tank Size: 75 Gallon (300 litre)
Water Conditions: 78-86° F, 25-30° C, KH 8-12, pH 6.0-7.5
Diet: Omnivore
Origin: Cambodia
Aquarium Type: Large Community bottom dweller

Notes:
Give these guys a good quality flake, sinking pellets and algae wafers. They also love fresh cucumber and veggies.

These loaches should be kept in groups of 5 or more and with other peaceful species: rasboras, barbs, corydoras, danios, catfish and other boisterous loaches.

Provide them with plenty of cover, caves, hiding places, plants and a fine substrate

Burmese Polkadot Loach

These loaches are very similar to the bengal loach and can be identified by their array of spots.

Scientific Name: Botia Kubotai
Care Level: Moderate
Temperament: Peaceful – bottom dweller
Maximum Size: 4" – 5" (12cm)
Minimum Tank Size: 50 Gallons (200 litres)
Water Conditions: 72-86° F, 23-30° C, KH 8-12, pH 6.0-7.5
Diet: Omnivore – offer them a good quality sinking pellet food
Origin: India
Aquarium Type: Community

Notes:
These loaches prefer tanks decorated in a natural style with fine substrate, stones and driftwood roots or branches. These fish also require plenty of cover in the form of live plants, rocks and terra cotta pots.

These guys should be kept in groups of a 5 or more and enjoy pellets and juicy pieces of cucumber.

These loaches seem compatible with most other peaceful fish.

Clown Loach

This is a wonderful loach, they are playful and entertaining. They can be easily identified by their bold black and gold stripes and scarlet fins.

Scientific Name: Chromobotia Macracanthus
Care Level: Moderate
Temperament: Peaceful - bottom dweller
Maximum Size: up to 12" (30cm)
Minimum Tank Size: 75 - 80 Gallons (300 litre)
Water Conditions: 76-86° F, 25-30° C, KH 8-12, pH 6.0-7.5
Diet: Omnivore
Origin: Indonesia
Aquarium Type: Large Community-Bottom-Dweller

Notes
They love being in groups of 5 or more, although I'd suggest having at least 10 or 12 in a large tank. They love to eat cucumber and good for controlling pest snails. They also love wormy foods and go mad over frozen bloodworm. They also like a good quality pellet food.

They love lots of hiding places, caves and well planted tanks with fine substrate. They have been known to nibble on delicate plants so make sure you select hardy plants when you set up your tank.

They seem to be compatible with most other peaceful species. livebearers, rasboras, barbs, corydoras, danios, catfish and other Loaches.

Dwarf Chain Loach

These loaches are very small and can be identified by their 'chain like' array of spots along the side of their body.

Scientific Name: Ambastaia Sidthimunki
Care Level: Moderate
Temperament: Semi-aggressive
Maximum Size: 2.5" (6cm)
Minimum Tank Size: 30 Gallon (120 litre)
Water Conditions: 76-86° F, 25-30° C, KH 8-12, pH 6.0-7.5
Diet: Omnivore – offer a good quality sinking pellet
Origin: Thailand
Aquarium Type: Community

Notes:
These Loaches are best in a well-planted tank. They remain fairly small and are best kept in groups of 3 or more with diffused lighting.

They love sinking foods with plenty of small foods such as freeze dried bloodworms, artemia and daphnia. They also love a bit of fresh cucumber now and again. They are also good for controlling pest snails.

They seem to be compatible with most species but they have been known to be aggressive at times and nip at other species.

Horse-face Loach

This loach is quite a fascinating looking species, and get be easily identified by its face that looks very similar to a horse's face.

Scientific Name: Acantopsis Choirorhynchos
Care Level: Moderate
Temperament: Peaceful but can become territorial
Maximum Size: 8" (20cm)
Minimum Tank Size: 50 Gallon   (200 litre)
Water Conditions: 79-86° F, 26-30° C, KH 3-5, pH 6.0-6.5
Diet: Omnivore
Origin: Southeast Asia
Aquarium Type: Community

Notes:
These loaches are best kept in groups of 5 or more and can be kept with danios, cyprinids and other loaches.

Because this loach may exhibit aggressive or territorial behaviour, these fish are best kept with species that tend to swim in the upper levels of the tank.

Give them a diet of high-quality sinking foods supplemented with frozen foods such as bloodworms, artemia and daphnia.

Kuhli Loach

The Kuhli Loach is long and thin and loves to dig, so make sure they have some nice sand somewhere in the tank.

Scientific Name: Pangio Kuhlii
Care Level: Moderate
Temperament: Peaceful
Maximum Size: 5" (12cm)
Minimum Tank Size: 50 Gallon   (200 litre)
Water Conditions: 79-86° F, 25-30° C, KH 3-5, pH 6.0-6.5
Diet: Carnivore
Origin: Indonesia
Aquarium Type: Community

Notes:
Largely nocturnal, these loaches are shy fish that like to hide among driftwood, plant roots, rocks, and caves.

They are peaceful fish that get along well with other peaceful tank mates.

Although it is a scavenger, this loach is largely carnivorous, preferring freeze-dried bloodworms and tubifex, as well as frozen foods of all types.

Skunk Loach

Also known as Hora's loach, the skunk loach is easily identified by its black markings along the top of its body much like a skunk

Scientific Name: Yasuhikotakia Morleti
Care Level: Moderate
Temperament: Peaceful but can be aggressive at times
Maximum Size: 4" (12cm)
Minimum Tank Size: 50 Gallon   (200 litre)
Water Conditions: 79-82° F, 25-27° C, KH 3-5, pH 6.0-6.5
Diet: Omnivore
Origin: Thailand
Aquarium Type: Community

Notes:
These loaches are best kept in groups of 5 or more but choose other tank mates carefully and try rasboras, danios, catfish and other loaches of similar size. Avoid slow moving fish with long fins as they tend to fin nip.

Give them fine substrate as they love to create burrows under rocks, also driftwood branches and some live plants with plenty of hiding places.

Feed them a varied diet of frozen foods and use a high-quality sinking pellet food.

Yoyo Loach

Also known as the Almora loach or Pakistani loach and is very similar to the bengal loach.

Scientific Name: Botia Almorhae
Care Level: Easy
Temperament: Peaceful
Maximum Size: 6" (15cm)
Minimum Tank Size: 50 Gallon   (200 litre)
Water Conditions: 72-82° F, 25-27° C, KH 8-12, pH 6.0-7.5
Diet: Omnivore
Origin: India
Aquarium Type: Community

Notes:
These loaches should be kept in groups of 5 and make great companions for small-medium sized robust species, such as some members of the danio and barb families.

You should give them a fine substrate as not to damage their barbels, and numerous hiding places should be provided: bogwood, caves, and aquatic plants with subdued lighting.

Feed them on a good quality sinking pellet. They also love cucumber and veggies now and again. These loaches will also eat pest snails in the tank.

Zebra Loach

Also known as the candy striped loach, the zebra loach is easily identified by its thin black stripes along the side of its body much like a zebra.

Scientific Name: Botia Striata
Care Level: Easy
Temperament: Peaceful
Maximum Size: 4" (10cm)
Minimum Tank Size: 40 Gallon   (150 litre)
Water Conditions: 73-80° F, 22-26° C, KH 3-5, pH 6.0-6.5
Diet: Omnivore
Origin: India
Aquarium Type: Community

Notes:
These loaches are best kept in groups of 5 or more and can be kept with rasboras, danios, catfish and other loaches.

They love a sandy substrate, smooth stones and driftwood roots or branches with plenty of hiding places

Give them a staple diet of high-quality sinking pellet foods with frozen foods such as bloodworms, daphnia and artemia. They also enjoy a bit of cucumber now and again and will eat pest snails in the tank.

Weather Loach

Also known as pond loach, Dojo Loach, or the Japanese Weather Loach, has a long thin body, and is usually gold/orange or brown/white with grey spots.

Scientific Name: Misgurnus Anguillicaudatus
Care Level: Moderate
Temperament: Peaceful
Maximum Size: 10" (25cm)
Minimum Tank Size: 50 Gallon (200 litre)
Water Conditions: 64-75° F, 17-24° C, KH 3-5, pH 6.0-8.0
Diet: Omnivore
Origin: East Asia
Aquarium Type: Cold water Community

Notes:
These loaches need a lower temperature than most other tropical fish so tank mates are limited and does better with cold water fish such as gold fish.

This fish needs plenty of space to move around, and a fine substrate as they love to dig and bury themselves up to the head. Do not use stones or course gravel.

They love sinking pellets, frozen bloodworm as well as live foods.

Cory Catfish

Cory Cats belong to the Callichthyidae family and are some of the most peaceful, entertaining scavengers for a freshwater aquarium, and will thrive in a wide range of water conditions.

These catfish are very efficient and energetic scavengers who remain relatively small; because of this, they are perfect for keeping the substrate clean in a smaller freshwater community aquarium.

These guys are usually compatible with most other peaceful bottom dwellers and fish of the same size. Don't mix them with aggressive fish.

Banded Corydoras

Also known as the Barbatus Cory and can be identified by its gold and black bands.

Scientific Name: Scleromystax Barbatus
Care Level: Moderate
Temperament: Peaceful although males can be territorial
Maximum Size: 5" (12cm)
Minimum Tank Size: 60 Gallon   (220 litre)
Water Conditions: 68-75° F, 20-23° C, KH 8-10, pH 6.8-7.2
Diet: Omnivore – offer a good sinking pellet
Origin: Brazil
Aquarium Type: Community

Notes:
These cories enjoy being in groups of 5 or more and prefer a well planted aquarium with plenty of cover and fine substrate.

They seem to get on with most other peaceful species, but not a good idea to mix with predatory or aggressive fish.

Feed them dried and frozen foods. Ensure algae wafers or spirulina are included in the diet.

Blackstripe Bondi Corydoras

These cories can be identified by the black stripe across the side of its body.

Scientific Name: Corydoras Bondi
Care Level: Moderate
Temperament: Peaceful
Maximum Size: 2" (5cm)
Minimum Tank Size: 15 Gallon (60 litre)
Water Conditions: 68-75° F, 20-23° C, KH 8-10, pH 6.8-7.2
Diet: Omnivore but prefers meaty foods
Origin: South America
Aquarium Type: Community

Notes:
These cories enjoy being in groups of 5 or more and prefer a well planted aquarium with plenty of cover and fine substrate.

They seem to get on with most other peaceful species and other cories, but not a good idea to mix with predatory or aggressive fish.

Feed them sinking algae pellets should be supplemented with flake food or other sinking foods like catfish pellets.

Blue Corydoras

Also known as Natterer's catfish, these cories are a beautiful blue shade with a deep blue stripe.

Scientific Name: Corydoras Nattereri
Care Level: Easy
Temperament: Peaceful
Maximum Size: 2" (5cm)
Minimum Tank Size: 15 Gallon   (60 litre)
Water Conditions: 68-75° F, 20-23° C, KH 8-10, pH 6.0-7.2
Diet: Omnivore – good quality sinking pellet
Origin: South America
Aquarium Type: Community

Notes:
These cories enjoy being in groups of 5 or more and prefer a well planted aquarium with plenty of cover and fine substrate.

They seem to get on with most other peaceful species and other cories, but not a good idea to mix with predatory or aggressive fish.

Feed them sinking algae pellets should be supplemented with flake food or other sinking foods like catfish pellets.

Bronze Corydoras

Sometimes called the lightspot corydoras or wavy catfish and is usually a beautiful green-brown colour.

Scientific Name: Corydoras Aeneus
Care Level: Easy
Temperament: Peaceful
Maximum Size: 3" (7cm)
Minimum Tank Size: 25 Gallon   (90 litre)
Water Conditions: 65-77° F, 18-25° C, KH 2-15, pH 6.0-7.5
Diet: Omnivore – offer a good quality sinking pellet
Origin: South America
Aquarium Type: Community

Notes:
These corys are best kept in groups of about 5 or more and can be kept with tetras, barbs, livebearers, cyprinids and dwarf cichlids.

Provide them with a well planted tank with plenty of hiding places and fine substrate

Feed them a diet of sinking pellets along with frozen foods such as brine shrimp and bloodworms. They also love a few blanched veggies now and again.

Dwarf Corydoras

Sometimes called the tail spot pygmy catfish, or micro catfish and is usually a white-olive colour.

Scientific Name: Corydoras Hastatus
Care Level: Easy
Temperament: Peaceful
Maximum Size: 1" (2.5cm)
Minimum Tank Size: 15 Gallon   (60 litre)
Water Conditions: 72-79° F, 22-26° C, KH 2-15, pH 6.0-7
Diet: Omnivore – good quality micro pellet
Origin: Amazon River
Aquarium Type: Community

Notes:
These corys are best kept in groups of about 5 or more and can be kept with similar sized fish, peaceful species.

This little guy prefers dimly lit, heavily planted tank decorated with fine substrate, pieces of bogwood and twisted roots, and some hiding places.

Any food offered must be small enough for its mouth. It will take dried foods, but these should be a small grade or ground down.

Hognosed Brochis

Hognose can be identified by its longer snout and head, and usually has a green colouring along its side.

Scientific Name: Corydoras Multiradiatus
Care Level: Easy
Temperament: Peaceful
Maximum Size: 4" (10cm)
Minimum Tank Size: 40 Gallon (150 litre)
Water Conditions: 68-75° F, 20-23° C, KH 8-10, pH 6.8-7.2
Diet: Omnivore
Origin: Amazon River
Aquarium Type: Community

Notes:
Well suited to the community tank with characins, cyprinids, anabantids, dwarf cichlids and other catfish.

Give them a fine substrate with a planted tank and plenty of cover.

Feed them a varied diet of sinking pellets or wafers along with frozen foods such as brine shrimp, tubifex worms and bloodworms. They also love a few blanched veggies.

Emerald Cory

This cory has an emerald green body with pink highlights on the lower parts and underbelly.

Scientific Name: Corydoras Splendens
Care Level: Easy
Temperament: Peaceful
Maximum Size: 3" (7cm)
Minimum Tank Size: 30 Gallons (100 litre)
Water Conditions: 68-75° F, 20-23° C, KH 8-10, pH 6.8-7.2
Diet: Omnivore
Origin: South America
Aquarium Type: Community

Notes:
This Cory is well suited to a community tank and is compatible with characins, cyprinids, anabantids, dwarf cichlids and other catfish.

Give them a well in a planted tank with plenty of cover and fine substrate and are best kept in groups of 5 or more.

They love a varied diet of sinking pellets along with frozen foods such as brine shrimp, tubifex worms and bloodworms. Also offer them some blanched veggies too.

Elegant Corydoras

These cories are silver to gold in colour with horizontal black dotted stripes that run from the back of the head to the tail of the fish.

Scientific Name: Corydoras Elegans
Care Level: Easy
Temperament: Peaceful although males can fight
Maximum Size: 3" (7cm)
Minimum Tank Size: 40 Gallon   (150 litre)
Water Conditions: 70-82° F, 21-27° C, KH 2-15, pH 6.0-7.5
Diet: Omnivore
Origin: Amazon River
Aquarium Type: Community

Notes:
These guys should be kept in groups of about 5 or more and can be kept with characins, cyprinids, anabantids, dwarf cichlids and other catfish.

Sometimes males can fight amongst themselves so provide a well planted tank with plenty of cover and hiding places with fine substrate.

Feed them a diet of sinking pellets and wafers along with a few blanched vegies now and again

Julii Corydoras

This cory has mottled black dots and stripes with a silver coloured body.

Scientific Name: Corydoras Julii
Care Level: Easy
Temperament: Peaceful
Maximum Size: 2.5" (6cm)
Minimum Tank Size: 30 Gallon (100 litre)
Water Conditions: 68-75° F, 20-23° C, KH 8-10, pH 6.8-7.2
Diet: Omnivore – good quality sinking pellet
Origin: Amazon River
Aquarium Type: Community

Notes:
These little cories should be kept in groups of about 5 or more and can be kept with characins, cyprinids, anabantids, dwarf cichlids and other catfish. Do not keep with large, aggressive fish.

Provide them with a well planted tank with plenty of cover and fine substrate.

Use a good quality sinking pellet or tablet as the staple diet. Sometimes they love some blanched veggies now and again.

Bandit Corydoras

Also known as the masked cory and has a black stripe across his eyes and a black stripe across the top of his back and dorsal fin much resembling a bandit's face mask.

Scientific Name: Corydoras Metae
Care Level: Easy
Temperament: Peaceful
Maximum Size: 2" (5cm)
Minimum Tank Size: 20 Gallons (75 litre)
Water Conditions: 72-78° F, 22-27° C, KH 2-15, pH 6.0-7.5
Diet: Omnivore
Origin: Colombia, South America
Aquarium Type: Community

Notes:
These little cories should be kept in groups of about 5 or more and can be kept with characins, cyprinids, anabantids, dwarf cichlids and other catfish. Do not keep with large, aggressive fish.

Provide them with a well planted tank with plenty of cover and fine substrate.

They enjoy a good quality micro sinking pellet or flake along with some blanched veggies now and again. They also love freeze dried bloodworms, chopped earthworm and brine shrimp.

Panda Corydoras

Very similar to the bandit cory and has a black stripe across his eyes with a black dorsal fin and patch near his tail fin resembling the markings of a panda.

Scientific Name: Corydoras Panda
Care Level: Easy
Temperament: Peaceful bottom dweller
Maximum Size: 2.5" (6cm)
Minimum Tank Size: 25 Gallon   (90 litre)
Water Conditions: 70-80° F, 21-26° C, KH 2-15, pH 6.0-7.5
Diet: Omnivore
Origin: Amazon River
Aquarium Type: Community

Notes:
These little cories should be kept in groups of about 5 or more and can be kept with characins, cyprinids, anabantids, dwarf cichlids and other catfish. Do not keep with large, aggressive fish.

Provide them with a well planted tank with plenty of cover and fine substrate.

They enjoy a good quality micro sinking pellet or flake along with some blanched veggies now and again. They also love freeze dried bloodworms, chopped earthworm and brine shrimp.

Peppered Corydoras

Also known as the mottled corydoras and can be identified with his grey markings.

Scientific Name: Corydoras Habrosus
Care Level: Easy
Temperament: Peaceful
Maximum Size: 3" (7cm)
Minimum Tank Size: 20 Gallons (75 litre)
Water Conditions: 72-80° F, 22-26° C, KH 2-12, pH 6.0-7.0
Diet: Omnivore
Origin: South America, Amazon
Aquarium Type: Community

Notes:
These cories love being in groups of at least 5. They should be kept in a well plated aquarium with plenty of cover and hiding places with fine substrate.

They seem to be compatible with most peaceful fish.

Feed them freeze-dried bloodworms and tubifex, sinking catfish pellets, flake food. They also enjoy some blanched veggies now and again.

Salt & Pepper Corydoras

The salt & pepper corydoras and can be identified with his small spotted black dots.

Scientific Name: Corydoras Paleatus
Care Level: Easy
Temperament: Peaceful
Maximum Size: 1" (2.5cm)
Minimum Tank Size: 15 Gallon (60 litre)
Water Conditions: 77-80° F, 25-26° C, KH 2-22, pH 6.0-8.0
Diet: Omnivore - good quality micro pellet/flake
Origin: South America
Aquarium Type: Community

Notes:
Provide these fish with a planted tank with plenty of cover and fine substrate. Keep in groups of 5 or more with similar sized fish, peaceful species.

This fish seems compatible with most other peaceful species and other bottom dwelling fish. Because of this fish's small size, do not keep with predatory species such as pictus catfish or any big fish.

These little fish will eat smaller flakes, micro pellets.

Schwartz's Catfish

The Schwartz corydoras can be identified with his small horizontal spotted black stripes on a bright silver body.

Scientific Name: Corydoras Schwartzi
Care Level: Easy
Temperament: Peaceful
Maximum Size: 2" (5cm)
Minimum Tank Size: 30 Gallons (100 litre)
Water Conditions: 72-79° F, 22-26° C, KH 2-12, pH 5.8-7.0
Diet: Omnivore
Origin: South America
Aquarium Type: Community

Notes:
This cory is best kept in groups of 5 or more and is well suited to a community tank with characins, cyprinids, anabantids, dwarf cichlids and other catfish.

Give them a planted tank with plenty of hiding places and cover with fine substrate

Feed them a varied diet of small sinking pellets or wafers along with frozen foods such as brine shrimp. They also enjoy a few blanched veggies now and again.

Sixray/False Corydoras

These cories are quite small and can be identified by its small black spots on a silver body.

Scientific Name: Corydoras Leucomelas
Care Level: Easy
Temperament: Peaceful
Maximum Size: 1.5" (3.5cm)
Minimum Tank Size: 15 Gallon   (60 litre)
Water Conditions: 72-75° F, 22-23° C, KH 8-10, pH 6.0-7.2
Diet: Omnivore – offer a good sinking small pellet or flake
Origin: South America
Aquarium Type: Community

Notes:
Also known as the false cory. This species should be kept in groups of 3 or more, in a planted aquarium with fine substrate and plenty of shelter.

They are compatible with most peaceful species and similar sized fish. Do not keep with predatory or aggressive species.

They will accept micro pellets and flakes.

Sterba's Corydoras

This cory has white spots on a black body and sometimes the spots form spotted stripes along the side of his body.

Scientific Name: Corydoras Sterbai
Care Level: Easy
Temperament: Peaceful
Maximum Size: 3" (7cm)
Minimum Tank Size: 30 Gallons (100 litre)
Water Conditions: 70-79° F, 21-26° C, KH 2-15, pH 6.0-7.8
Diet: Omnivore
Origin: Brazil, Amazon, South America
Aquarium Type: Community

Notes:
This cory is best kept in groups of 5 or more and is well suited to a community tank with characins, cyprinids, anabantids, dwarf cichlids and other catfish.

Provide a well planted tank with plenty of cover and fine substrate

Offer them dried, flake, frozen foods. Feed a quality flake and pellet food as well as frozen brine.

Albino Corydoras

This cory is yellow to orange in colour with hints of red around his head.

Scientific Name: Corydoras Aeneus Albino
Care Level: Easy
Temperament: Peaceful
Maximum Size: 3" (7cm)
Minimum Tank Size: 25 Gallon   (90 litre)
Water Conditions: 72-79° F, 22-26° C, KH 2-15, pH 6.0-7.0
Diet: Omnivore – offer a good quality sinking pellet
Origin: South America
Aquarium Type: Community

Notes:
These corys are best kept in groups of about 5 or more and can be kept with tetras, barbs, livebearers, cyprinids and dwarf cichlids.

Provide them with a well planted tank with plenty of hiding places and fine substrate

Feed them a diet of sinking pellets along with frozen foods such as brine shrimp and bloodworms. They also love a few blanched veggies now and again.

Plecos

Plecostomus, Pleco, Pleccy or just Plec. These fish have specially adapted mouthparts, enabling them to feed off the substrate, rocks or glass and belong to the Loricariidae family. They are great for keeping algae at bay in an aquarium.

Most plecs are peaceful fish and prefer to rest or slowly graze over the aquarium bottom.

Keep in mind that some plecs can grow very large and outgrow most home aquariums.

Plecs are generally peaceful, however some larger species will become more aggressive with age.

Some species it is wise to only have one as they can become aggressive to one another if they were not raised together.

Some plecs will destroy live plants, so make sure plants are either artificial or a hardy species.

Bristlenose Plec

Bristlenose can be identified by small bristles around his mouth and nose and yellow/white spots on a black body.

Scientific Name: Ancistrus
Care Level: Easy
Temperament: Peaceful
Maximum Size: 4" - 5" (10cm)
Minimum Tank Size: 30 Gallons (100 litre)
Water Conditions: 74-82° F, 23-28° C, KH 6-10, pH 6.0-7.5
Diet: Omnivore but preferably herbivore
Origin: South America, Amazon
Aquarium Type: Community

Notes:
This is a lovely little plec, he loves lots of shelter and hiding places, prefers a planted tank and requires some kind of bogwood or driftwood as they love to gnaw at it and helps their digestion.

He loves cucumber and algae wafers and is great for cleaning algae off the inside of the tank.

He can usually exist on his own and is compatible with most other peaceful species. Has been known to become territorial at times.

Common Plec

These guys can typically be purchased when they're about 3" but often grow up to a monstrous 24"!!

Scientific Name: Hypostomus Plecostomus
Care Level: Moderate
Temperament: Peaceful but can become aggressive with age
Maximum Size: up to 24" (60cm)
Minimum Tank Size: 80-100 Gallon (400 litre)
Water Conditions: 74-82° F, 23-27° C, KH 6-10, pH 6.0-7.5
Diet: Omnivore but mainly herbivorous
Origin: Indonesia
Aquarium Type: Non-Community

Notes:
They become more aggressive with age and are best kept individually in tanks. Such fish should only be considered for the largest aquariums.

While juveniles are generally an excellent community fish, any adult plecos should be kept in a semi-aggressive tank, and should never be kept with any other common plecos.

As well as feeding him with pellets and tank algae. It should also be fed algae wafers, zucchini/courgette, cucumber, lettuce, peas, and melon, and any fruit or vegetable will do, as well. They also can eat shrimp, pellets, and flake fish food.

Gold Nugget Plec

These plecs have beautiful gold/yellow stripes along the edges of the dorsal and tail fins with gold spots and black body.

Scientific Name: Baryancistrus (L-18)
Care Level: Moderate
Temperament: Peaceful but can be territorial
Maximum Size: 6" (15cm)
Minimum Tank Size: 55 Gallons (200 litre)
Water Conditions: 73-80° F, 22-26° C, KH 8-10, pH 6.5-7.0
Diet: Omnivore
Origin: South America
Aquarium Type: Community

Notes:
Only keep one of these guys in a tank as they have been known to fight to the death. They are well-suited to the large community tank and can be kept with characins, cichlids, and loaches etc.

Give them a well planted tank with plenty of hiding places with smooth or fine substrate.

Offer him a high-quality sinking pellet or wafer along with frozen foods such as brine shrimp, prawns and bloodworms. Cucumber is always a favourite.

Leopard Sailfin Plec

Another species that grows very large and can be identified by its leopard spot body and large dorsal fin.

Scientific Name: Pterygoplichthys Gibbiceps
Care Level: Easy
Temperament: Peaceful
Maximum Size: up to 24" (60cm)
Minimum Tank Size: 80-100 Gallon (400 litre)
Water Conditions: 74-80° F, 23-26° C, KH 6-10, pH 6.5-7.5
Diet: Omnivore
Origin: Amazon, South America
Aquarium Type: Large-Bottom-Dweller

Notes:
This pleco will do well in a larger aquarium with a sandy or gravel substrate, larger pieces of driftwood, large rocks and some plants. They will also appreciate some plants, wood or rocks that create a covered or shaded area within the aquarium so that they can escape the bright aquarium lights when needed.

Their large adult size can be destructive to aquariums that are heavily planted as they may uproot or damage sensitive plants when the swim around.

They prefer a diet of sinking flake or pellet foods, naturally occurring algae or algae wafers, sinking carnivore pellets and other various flake, freeze-dried and pellet foods that are fed to other tank mates.

Zebra Plec

This plec has a beautiful black and white striped body and doesn't grow as large as other species of plec

Scientific Name: Hypancistrus Zebra (L-46)
Care Level: Moderate
Temperament: Peaceful and timid
Maximum Size: 4" (10cm)
Minimum Tank Size: 30 Gallon   (100 litre)
Water Conditions: 77-86° F, 25-30° C, KH 2-10, pH 6.5-7.5
Diet: Omnivore – good quality sinking pellet or wafer
Aquarium Type: Community

Notes:
Zebra Plecy is a shy fish and should not be kept with other bottom dwelling fish that will compete for food and should be kept with species of similar temperament.

He likes a tank with plenty of plant cover, driftwood and hiding places with fine substrate and subdued lighting.

He enjoys a high quality flake food, sinking carnivore pellets, and frozen or freeze-dried bloodworms tubifex and brine shrimp, as well as sinking algae wafers.

Albino Sailfin Plec

This plec is orange/yellow in appearance and has been known to grow up to 24" but will normally grow to half that size in a home aquarium

Scientific Name: Pterygoplichthys Gibbiceps Albino
Care Level: Easy
Temperament: Peaceful
Maximum Size: usually between 7" and 12" (17cm - 30cm)
Minimum Tank Size: 55 Gallons (200 litre)
Water Conditions: 69-78° F, 20-25° C, KH 6-10, pH 6.5-7.5
Diet: Omnivore
Origin: Amazon, South America
Aquarium Type: Large-Bottom-Dweller

Notes:
Keen him in a larger aquarium with a sandy or gravel substrate, larger pieces of driftwood, large rocks and some plants. They will also appreciate some plants, wood or rocks that create a covered or shaded area within the aquarium so that they can escape the bright aquarium lights when needed.

Their large adult size can be destructive to aquariums that are heavily planted as they may uproot or damage sensitive plants when the swim around.

They prefer a diet of sinking flake or pellet foods, naturally occurring algae or algae wafers, veg, sinking carnivore pellets and other various flake, freeze-dried and pellet foods that are fed to other tank mates.

Royal Plec

The royal plec has black steaks on a mossy green coloured truncated body that looks a bit like a hump.

Scientific Name: Panaque Nigrolineatus (L-027)
Care Level: Easy
Temperament: Peaceful
Maximum Size: 12" (30cm)
Minimum Tank Size: 55 Gallons (200 litre)
Water Conditions: 74-79° F, 23-26° C, KH 6-10, pH 6.5-7.5
Diet: Omnivore
Origin: South America
Aquarium Type: Large-Bottom-Dweller

Notes:
Give them sandy or gravel substrate, larger pieces of driftwood, large rocks and some plants. They will also appreciate some plants, wood or rocks that create a covered or shaded area within the aquarium so that they can escape the bright aquarium lights when needed.

They prefer a diet of sinking flake or pellet foods, naturally occurring algae or algae wafers, veg, sinking carnivore pellets and other various flake, freeze-dried and pellet foods that are fed to other tank mates.

Blue Phantom Plec

This strikingly beautiful fish with blue/white spots on a dark grey body, originates from the Orinoco River Basin in Venezuela.

Scientific Name: Hemiancistrus Specie (L-128)
Care Level: Moderate
Temperament: Peaceful
Maximum Size: 7" (17cm)
Minimum Tank Size: 30 Gallon (100 litre)
Water Conditions: 72-77° F, 22-25° C, KH 6-16, pH 6.0-7.5
Diet: Omnivore
Origin: South America
Aquarium Type: Community

Notes:
Give them sandy or gravel substrate, larger pieces of driftwood, large rocks and some plants that create a covered or shaded area within the aquarium so that they can escape the bright aquarium lights when needed.

They seem compatible with most other peaceful species.

They prefer a diet of sinking flake or pellet foods, naturally occurring algae or algae wafers, veg, sinking carnivore pellets and other various flake, freeze-dried and pellet foods that are fed to other tank mates.

Clown Plec

This plec has yellow stripes on a black-brown body and originates from South America.

Scientific Name: Panaque Maccus (L-162)
Care Level: Easy
Temperament: Peaceful
Maximum Size: 4" (17cm)
Minimum Tank Size: 30 Gallon (100 litre)
Water Conditions: 75-82° F, 24-28°C, KH 6-10, pH 6.5-7.5
Diet: Omnivore
Origin: South America
Aquarium Type: Community

Notes:
Give them sandy or gravel substrate. They will also appreciate some plants, wood or rocks that create a covered or shaded area within the aquarium so that they can escape the bright aquarium lights when needed.

They seem compatible with most other peaceful species.

They prefer a diet of sinking flake or pellet foods, naturally occurring algae or algae wafers, veg, sinking carnivore pellets and other various flake, freeze-dried and pellet foods that are fed to other tank mates.

Chapter 6

Other Catfish

Named for their prominent barbels, which resemble a cat's whiskers.

Most catfish are bottom feeders, prefer to be in groups, like fine gravel and plenty of hiding spots.

Otocinclus Catfish

A small catfish that loves to eat algae and can be identified by his back stripe across his body and a small sucker mouth.

Scientific Name: Otocinclus Affinis
Care Level: Easy
Temperament: Peaceful
Maximum Size: 2" (5cm)
Minimum Tank Size: 30 Gallon   (100 litre)
Water Conditions: 77-86° F, 25-30° C, KH 6-10, pH 6.5-7.5
Diet: Herbivore – good quality algae wafer
Origin: South America
Aquarium Type: Community

Notes:
This little guy is an attractive and functional addition to any freshwater aquarium and he will continually graze on the algae in the tank.

The prefer a well planted aquarium with rocks and hiding places, bogwood and should be kept in groups of 3 or more

This fish will graze on algae but this should be supplemented with a good quality algae wafer or vegetable based flake or pellet food.

Panda Garra

The most common Panda Garra species has bands of dark brown and yellow markings

Scientific Name: Garra Flavatra
Care Level: Moderate
Temperament: Peaceful
Maximum Size: 3" (7cm)
Minimum Tank Size: 30 Gallon (100 litre)
Water Conditions: 72-77° F, 22-25° C, KH 6-10, pH 6.5-7.5
Diet: Omnivore
Origin: Indonesia
Aquarium Type: Community

Notes:
This little guy is well suited to a community aquarium and gets on well with most peaceful species and should be kept in groups of 3 or more.

They appreciate well planted tanks with lots of hiding places, fine substrate and medium lighting and a strong current so make sure your filter has a power head.

This fish is omnivorous and its diet should consist of prepared algae flake food or algae wafers as well as frozen or freeze-dried foods. The occasional addition of bloodworms or tubifex worms are also enjoyed as well as blanched vegies now and again with a cucumber treat.

Pictus Catfish

Pictus usually has dark black spots on a white/grey body with very long 'whiskers'.

Scientific Name: Pimelodus Pictus
Care Level: Moderate
Temperament: Peaceful; will eat fish small enough to fit in its mouth
Maximum Size: 6" (15cm)
Minimum Tank Size: 55 Gallon   (200 litre)
Water Conditions: 71-81° F, 21-27° C, KH 6-10, pH 6.0-7.5
Diet: Omnivore – use sinking pellet
Origin: Amazon river
Aquarium Type: Community

Notes:
These catfish are very appealing when small, but may grow somewhat large. Their mouths look small, but may eat smaller fish, such as neons, guppies etc, as they can open their mouths very wide. Rainbowfish, medium to large-sized characins, cyprinids and tough catfish such as Loricariids or Doradids are suitable tankmates

Pictus will appreciate a tank that is dimly lit and heavily planted with plenty of rocks, caves, and driftwood. Plants should be hardy. These guys are usually out at night and can be predatory but will usually co-exist with most species of similar size.

Feed him sinking wafers, pellets, frozen bloodworms, etc

Whiptail Catfish

Whiptails can be identified by their thin body with long dorsal fins and tail fins and sometimes known as the twig or stick catfish.

Scientific Name: Rineloricaria
Care Level: Easy
Temperament: Peaceful
Maximum Size: 5" (12cm)
Minimum Tank Size: 55 Gallon (200 litre)
Water Conditions: 68-77° F, 20-25° C, KH 4-10, pH 6.5-7.0
Diet: Omnivore
Origin: Brazil
Aquarium Type: Community

Notes:
Whiptails are very peaceful, interesting, remain relatively small, and are quite hardy and well suited to community aquariums with other non-aggressive fish.

They prefer well planted tanks with plenty of cover and fine substrate with diffused lighting. They love algae and bogwood

Feed them a variety of vegetable foods such as lettuce, peas, courgette/zucchini, blanched spinach, along with sinking a good quality sinking pellet food. They will graze algae.

Featherfin Catfish

Also known as the Featherfin Squeaker, or lace catfish and usually have a light brown body with dark spots and long barbal 'whiskers'.

Scientific Name: Synodontis Eupterus
Care Level: Easy
Temperament: Peaceful
Maximum Size: 6" (15cm)
Minimum Tank Size: 55 Gallon   (200 litre)
Water Conditions: 68-77° F, 20-25° C, KH 8-10, pH 6.5-7.0
Diet: Omnivore
Origin: Africa
Aquarium Type: Community

Notes:
This little guy is peaceful and will not normally eat much smaller fish, He can be little boisterous so he is best mixed with medium-large fish or fish of the same size.

Give him plenty of dark hiding places so he can retreat, make sure the substrate is fine with no sharp bits so he doesn't damage his barbels. He is a good aquarium fish with plenty of character.

Feed him sinking pellets, live or frozen foods.

Striped Raphael

Also known as the, thorny catfish or talking catfish because he produces clicks, and squeaks.

Scientific Name: Platyodras Armatulus
Care Level: Easy but be aware of spiky fins
Temperament: Peaceful
Maximum Size: 7" (18cm)
Minimum Tank Size: 40 Gallon   (150 litre)
Water Conditions: 75-80° F, 23-26° C, KH 4-10, pH 6.5-7.0
Diet: Omnivore
Origin: Columbia
Aquarium Type: Community

Notes:
This fish is compatible most other species, however do not keep him with any fish that can fit in his mouth.

Raphael loves to burrow so give him fine sand substrate and plenty of hiding places in the tank.

He enjoys the usual sinking catfish pellets

Banjo Catfish

Known for his distinctive 'banjo' shape, this fish is usually brown in colour and has a long thin tail.

Scientific Name: Bunocephalus Coracoideus
Care Level: Moderate
Temperament: Peaceful
Maximum Size: 6" (15cm)
Minimum Tank Size: 55 Gallon   (200 litre)
Water Conditions: 68-77° F, 20-25° C, KH 8-10, pH 6.5-7.0
Diet: Omnivore
Origin: Brazil
Aquarium Type: Community

Notes:
Give banjo a sand substrate as they like to burrow. Provide them with subdued lighting, bits of bogwood and plenty of caves and hiding places.

This fish seems to be compatible with most species of tetra and cichlids, cories, loaches, and can be housed singly or as a group.

Chapter 7

Characins

Characins belong to the Characidae family and are active schooling fish that work well in the peaceful community aquarium.

It is ideal to keep six or more fish of the same tetra species in the aquarium and can form spectacular displays.

Characins do best in a well-planted aquarium with moderate lighting.

Black Phantom Tetra

These tetras are light grey in with a black patch, surrounded by iridescent silver.

Scientific Name: Hyphessobrycon Megalopterus
Care Level: Easy
Temperament: Peaceful
Maximum Size: 2" (5cm)
Minimum Tank Size: 12 Gallons (50 litre)
Water Conditions: 72-82° F, 22-27° C, KH 4-8, pH 6.0-7.5
Diet: Omnivore – provide a good flake food
Origin: Brazil
Aquarium Type: Community

Notes:
These fish should be kept in large schools of at least 5. They appreciate a well planted tank with plenty of cover.

Suitable tank mates should include other peaceful tropical species similar in size and disposition. When keeping black phantom tetra with barb species like tiger barbs, it is important to keep a group of the Barbs as they naturally nip at each other.

They enjoy a quality flake food, brine shrimp, daphnia, freeze-dried tubifex or blood worms and micro pellets

Black Neon Tetra

This tetra has adjacent horizontal stripes of white and black with hints of red and yellow.

Scientific Name: Hyphessobrycon Herbertaxelrodi
Care Level: Easy
Temperament: Peaceful
Maximum Size: 1.5" (4cm)
Minimum Tank Size: 12 Gallons (50 litre)
Water Conditions: 72-79° F, KH 4-8, pH 5.5-7.0
Diet: Omnivore
Origin: Brazilian Amazon
Aquarium Type: Community

Notes:
These fish should be kept in schools of at least 5 and can be housed with tank mates such as other tetra, hatchet fish, cory cats, rasbora, gourami, peaceful barb species and some smaller cichlids like rams cichlids.

The Black Neon Tetra will have a difficult time competing with boisterous species like many barb species and danio species for food and territory. Also because of their small adult size, this fish is not well suited for aquariums with angelfish or larger shark or catfish species who will often eat the sleeping tetra during the night time hours.

Provide them with a well planted tank and plenty of cover and will readily accept a variety of flake, crisp, freeze-dried and frozen foods

Bleeding Heart Tetra

This tetra can be identified by its red patch near the pectoral fins with a black and white patch on the dorsal fin.

Scientific Name: Hyphessobrycon Erythrostigma
Care Level: Easy
Temperament: Peaceful
Maximum Size: 2" (5cm)
Minimum Tank Size: 20 Gallons (80 litre)
Water Conditions: 73-81° F, 22-27° C, KH 4-10, pH 5.5-7.0
Diet: Omnivore
Origin: Amazon, Brazil, Peru, Colombia
Aquarium Type: Community

Notes:
These fish should be kept in large schools of at least 5. They appreciate a well planted tank with plenty of cover.

Tank mates should include other peaceful tropical community species, peaceful bottom dwellers and peaceful dwarf cichlid species.

Provide them with a well planted tank and plenty of cover and will readily accept a variety of flake, crisp, freeze-dried and frozen foods

Blood-fin Tetra

This tetra has a red colouration on the all its fins with a long silver body.

Scientific Name: Aphyocharax Anisitsi
Care Level: Easy
Temperament: Peaceful
Maximum Size: 2" (5cm)
Minimum Tank Size: 20 Gallons (80 litre)
Water Conditions: 73-81° F, 22-27° C, KH 4-10, pH 5.5-7.0
Diet: Omnivore
Origin: Amazon, Brazil, Peru, Colombia
Aquarium Type: Community

Notes:
These fish should be kept in large schools of at least 5. They appreciate a well planted tank with plenty of cover.

Tank mates should include other peaceful tropical community species, peaceful bottom dwellers and peaceful dwarf cichlid species.

Provide them with a well planted tank and plenty of cover and will readily accept a variety of flake, crisp, freeze-dried and frozen foods

Buenos Aires Tetra

This tetra has a silver coloured body, with red-tipped fins and a black marking on the tail fin.

Scientific Name: Hyphessobrycon Anisitsi
Care Level: Easy
Temperament: Peaceful but can be aggressive
Maximum Size: 4" (10cm)
Minimum Tank Size: 30 Gallons (100 litre)
Water Conditions: 64-82° F, 17-27° C, KH 12-30, pH 7.0-8.3
Diet: Omnivore
Origin: South America
Aquarium Type: Community

Notes:
These fish are a bit more aggressive than some of the smaller Tetra species, but are still generally quite peaceful towards fish of similar size. They are known to eat some species of aquatic plants, but should not pose too much of a threat to a larger established and thriving planted aquarium.

Keep them in a group of at least 5 and provide them with a well planted tank with plenty of cover.

They will readily accept a variety of flake, crisp, freeze-dried and frozen foods

Congo Tetra

This tetra has blue colouring on top transitioning to red through the middle, to yellow-gold, and back just above the belly.

Scientific Name: Phenacogrammus Interruptus
Care Level: Moderate
Temperament: Peaceful
Maximum Size: 3" (7cm)
Minimum Tank Size: 30 Gallons (100 litre)
Water Conditions: 74-84° F, 23-28° C, KH 4-10, pH 6.0-7.5
Diet: Omnivore
Origin: Congo, Zaire
Family: Alestidae
Aquarium Type: Community

Notes:
Keep them in a group of at least 6 and provide them with a well planted tank with plenty of cover. Mix 2 or 3 females to 1 male or keep all males.

They will readily accept a variety of flake, crisp, freeze-dried and frozen foods

Emperor Tetra

This tetra has a three pronged tail with the medial black stripe along the side of its body.

Scientific Name: Nematobrycon Palmeri
Care Level: Easy
Temperament: Peaceful
Maximum Size: 2" (5cm)
Minimum Tank Size: 30 Gallons (100 litre)
Water Conditions: 74-82° F, 23-27° C, KH 4-10, pH 5.5-7.0
Diet: Omnivore
Origin: Rio San Juan, Rio Atrato, Colombia
Aquarium Type: Community

Notes:
These fish large enough and can be kept with angelfish, gourami, smaller catfish and sharks species, they are also very peaceful and will not harm other smaller or delicate tank mates.

Keep them in a group of at least 5 and provide them with a well planted tank with plenty of cover.

They will readily accept a variety of flake, crisp, freeze-dried and frozen foods

Glowlight Tetra

This fish is silver in colour with a bright iridescent orange to red stripe across its body.

Scientific Name: Hemigrammus Erythrozonus
Care Level: Easy
Temperament: Peaceful
Maximum Size: 2" (5cm)
Minimum Tank Size: 10 Gallons (40 litre)
Water Conditions: 72-78° F, 22-25° C, KH 4-8, pH 5.5-7.0
Diet: Omnivore
Origin: South America
Aquarium Type: Community

Notes:
This is a very peaceful species that should only be kept in peaceful tropical community aquariums with other small to medium sized peaceful community species

Keep them in a group of at least 5 and provide them with a well planted tank with plenty of cover.

They will readily accept a variety of flake, crisp, freeze-dried and frozen foods

Golden Pristella Tetra

Also known as the x-ray fish and has a semi translucent body with black and yellow markings on its dorsal fin.

Scientific Name: Pristella Maxillaris
Care Level: Easy
Temperament: Peaceful
Maximum Size: 2" (5cm)
Minimum Tank Size: 10 Gallons (40 litre)
Water Conditions: 72-79° F, 22-26° C, KH 4-8, pH 5.5-7.0
Diet: Omnivore
Origin: Brazilian Amazon
Aquarium Type: Community

Notes:
Suitable for very peaceful community aquariums that does not have semi-aggressive species like angelfish, catfish and barbs or fish that are big enough to eat them.

They can form a spectacular display if kept in large groups with at least 5. Provide them with a well planted tank with plenty of cover.

They will readily accept a variety of flake, crisp, freeze-dried and frozen foods

Lemon Tetra

This tetra's fins are marked with black and yellow and has a translucent yellow body.

Scientific Name: Hyphessobrycon Pulchripinnis
Care Level: Easy
Temperament: Peaceful
Maximum Size: 2" (5cm)
Minimum Tank Size: 10 Gallons (40 litre)
Water Conditions: 72-79° F, 22-26° C, KH 4-8, pH 5.5-7.0
Diet: Omnivore
Origin: Brazilian Amazon
Aquarium Type: Community

Notes:
Suitable for very peaceful community aquariums that does not have semi-aggressive species like angelfish, catfish and barbs or fish that are big enough to eat them.

They can form a spectacular display if kept in large groups with at least 5. Provide them with a well planted tank with plenty of cover. Make sure you have a good cover as these fish have been known to jump.

They will readily accept a variety of flake, crisp, freeze-dried and frozen foods

Neon Tetra

This tetra has a light-blue back over a silver-white abdomen with a blue and red stripe along its side.

Scientific Name: Paracheirodon Innesi
Care Level: Easy
Temperament: Peaceful
Maximum Size: 1.5" (4cm)
Minimum Tank Size: 10 Gallons (40 litre)
Water Conditions: 72-79° F, 22-26° C, KH 4-8, pH 5.5-7.0
Diet: Omnivore
Origin: Brazilian Amazon
Aquarium Type: Community

Notes:
This fish is only suitable for very peaceful community aquariums that does not have semi-aggressive species like angelfish, catfish and barbs or fish that are big enough to eat the neons.

They can form a spectacular display if kept in large groups with at least 5. Try 20 in a large tank for a really colourful display.

Provide them with a well planted tank with plenty of cover.

They will readily accept a variety of flake, crisp, freeze-dried and frozen foods

Penguin Tetra

These tetras are pale gold in colour, and have a black stripe across its body that extends down the bottom half of the tail fin.

Scientific Name:
Care Level: Easy
Temperament: Peaceful can be aggressive and fin nip
Maximum Size: 3" (7cm)
Minimum Tank Size: 20 Gallons (80 litre)
Water Conditions: 64-82° F, 16-27° C, KH 4-8, pH 5.8-8.5
Diet: Omnivore
Origin: South America, Amazon
Aquarium Type: Community

Notes:
Keep them in a group of at least 5 and provide them with a well planted tank with plenty of cover.

Do not keep with large finned fish such as bettas and guppies as these guys can't resist nipping at the large tail fins.

They will readily accept a variety of flake, crisp, freeze-dried and frozen foods

Red-eye Tetra

This tetra has a bright silver body accented by a white-edged black basal half of the tail and a thin red circle around its eye.

Scientific Name: Thayeria Boehlkei
Care Level: Easy
Temperament: Peaceful
Maximum Size: 3" (7cm)
Minimum Tank Size: 30 Gallons (100 litre)
Water Conditions: 72-80° F, 22-26° C, KH 4-8, pH 6.0-8.
Diet: Omnivore
Origin: Brazil, Paraguay and Argentina
Aquarium Type: Community

Notes:
Keep them in a group of at least 5 and provide them with a well planted tank with plenty of cover.

This fish will generally coexist with most all other community fish species

They will readily accept a variety of flake, crisp, freeze-dried and frozen foods

Red Phantom Tetra

The fish has a round black spot behind the gill-plate, a black band on the dorsal fin that is bordered above and below by creamy-white.

Scientific Name: Hyphessobrycon Sweglesi
Care Level: Easy
Temperament: Peaceful
Maximum Size: 2" (5cm)
Minimum Tank Size: 10 Gallons (40 litre)
Water Conditions: 72-82° F, 22-27° C, KH 4-8, pH 6.0-7.5
Diet: Omnivore – provide a good flake food
Origin: Brazil
Aquarium Type: Community

Notes:
These fish should be kept in large schools of at least 5. They appreciate a well planted tank with plenty of cover.

Suitable tank mates should include other peaceful tropical species similar in size and disposition. When keeping red phantom tetra with barb species like tiger barbs, it is important to keep a group of the Barbs as they naturally nip at each other.

They enjoy a quality flake food, brine shrimp, daphnia, freeze-dried tubifex or blood worms and micro pellets

Rummy Nose Tetra

This tetra is a torpedo-shaped fish with black and white spot markings on its tail and bright red colouring around its mouth and eyes.

Scientific Name: Hemigrammus Rhodostomus
Care Level: Easy
Temperament: Peaceful
Maximum Size: 2" (5cm)
Minimum Tank Size: 10 Gallons (40 litre)
Water Conditions: 72-77° F, 22-25° C, pH 5.5-7.0, KH 2-6
Diet: Omnivore
Origin: South America
Aquarium Type: Community

Notes:
Rummy nose tetras prefer an aquarium with plenty of vegetation and/or root or other drift woods. While an attractive fish in their own right, Rummy Nose Tetra really stand out when get in good sized groups of 8 or more individuals.

This fish will generally coexist with most all other community fish species

They will readily accept a variety of flake, crisp, freeze-dried and frozen foods

Serpae Tetra

Also known as long fin red minor tetra, long fin serpae tetra and, long fin blood tetra, and has a red body with a black spot near their eye.

Scientific Name: Hyphessobrycon Serpae
Care Level: Easy
Temperament: Peaceful
Maximum Size: 2" (5cm)
Minimum Tank Size: 20 Gallons (80 litre)
Water Conditions: 72-82° F, 22-27° C, KH 4-8, pH 6.0-7.5
Diet: Omnivore
Origin: South America
Aquarium Type: Community

Notes:
Keep them in a group of at least 5 and provide them with a well planted tank with plenty of cover.

They do best with tank mates that are peaceful. May nip the fins of guppies or betta fish.

They will readily accept a variety of flake, crisp, freeze-dried and frozen foods

Silver Dollar

These fish are usually bright silver in colour with pale fins and wide flat bodies.

Scientific Name: Metynnis Argenteus
Temperament: Peaceful but can be aggressive when feeding.
Maximum Size: 6" (15cm)
Minimum Tank Size: 55 Gallons (200 litre)
Water Conditions: 72-77° F, 22-25° C, KH 4-8, pH 5.0-7.0
Diet: Herbivore
Origin: South America
Aquarium Type: Community

Notes:
These fish are a lively schooling fish and best kept in groups of five or more. Set up your tank with plenty of rocks, plants, and driftwood. Make sure they have hiding places to retreat.

Silver Dollars are best kept in tanks with fish that can't fit in their mouths.

Labyrinth Fish

Most Labyrinth fish or anabantoids are surface air breathers and are part of the Osphronemidae family. A common species being gouramis which make a wonderful addition to the passive community aquarium adding brilliant colour and diversity.

Large species are very graceful swimmers that have unique colouration, and work best in the semi-aggressive community aquarium.

Chocolate Gourami

These fish are dark brown in colour with golden bands running down the sides of their bodies.

Scientific Name: Sphaerichthys Osphromenoides
Care Level: Difficult due to susceptibility to disease and delicate nature
Temperament: Peaceful
Maximum Size: 3" (7cm)
Minimum Tank Size: 30 Gallons (100 litre)
Water Conditions: 75-86° F, 23-29° C, KH 2-4, pH 6.0-7.6
Diet: Omnivore
Aquarium Type: Community

Notes:
This is a very delicate fish as it can be prone to bacteria and skin parasites, so good water quality is essential.

This fish prefers a well-established, densely tank, with dark substrate and requires frequent water changes. They do best if kept in pairs and are compatible with other peaceful fish.

Feed them an algae-based flake food, along with freeze-dried bloodworms, tubifex, and brine shrimp.

Dwarf Gourami

This gourami has vertical stripes of alternating blue and red colours while females are a silvery color.

Scientific Name: Colisa Lalia
Care Level: Easy
Temperament: Peaceful
Maximum Size: 2-4" (10cm)
Minimum Tank Size: 10 Gallons (40 litre)
Water Conditions: 72-82° F, 22-27° C, KH 5-20, pH 6.0-8.0
Diet: Omnivore
Aquarium Type: Community

Notes:
This fish will appreciate dark fine substrates and plenty of live plants and will bring out the brilliant colouration of the gourami.

Keep 3 or more and should not be kept with large, aggressive fish, but are compatible with other small, peaceful fish as well as fellow gouramis.

These fish like both algae-based foods as well as meaty foods. An algae-based flake food, along with freeze-dried bloodworms and tubifex.

Giant Gourami

This gourami is pale to golden yellow in colour, with silvery, pale blue stripes running vertically along its body.

Scientific Name: Osphronemus Goramy
Care Level: Easy
Temperament: Semi-aggressive
Maximum Size: 16" (40cm)
Minimum Tank Size: 90 Gallons (400 litre)
Water Conditions: 68-86° F, 20-30° C, KH 5-25, pH 6.0-8.0
Diet: Omnivore
Aquarium Type: Community

Notes:
These giants should only be considered for large aquarium setups and are compatible with silver dollars, knife fish and plecos

Provide live plants, rocks, driftwood in their tank.

He enjoys a pellet food supplemented with frozen blood worms or brine shrimp, also vegetables like spinach or lettuce, earthworms

Paradise Fish

This fish usually has red and blue markings along its body and tends to be brightly coloured.

Scientific Name: Macropodus Opercularis
Care Level: Easy
Temperament: Semi-aggressive
Maximum Size: 4" (10cm)
Minimum Tank Size: 30 Gallons (100 litre)
Water Conditions: 64-79° F, 17-26° C, KH 4-18, pH 6.0-8.0
Diet: Omnivore
Aquarium Type: Community

Notes:
This fish requires a large aquarium with lots of hiding places and can be territorial. For this reason, it should only be kept with other large, semi-aggressive fish.

Only keep one adult male as 2 will fight to the death much like the bettas.

This fish loves both algae-based foods as well as meaty foods. An algae-based flake food, along with freeze-dried bloodworms and tubifex.

Pearl Gourami

This fish is brownish-silver colour, covered in a pearl-like pattern with a distinct black line running from the eye to the tail.

Scientific Name: Trichopodus Leerii
Care Level: Easy
Temperament: Peaceful
Maximum Size: 4" (10cm)
Minimum Tank Size: 30 Gallons (100 litre)
Water Conditions: 74-86° F, 23-30° C, KH 5-18, pH 6.5-8.0
Diet: Omnivore
Aquarium Type: Community

Notes:
This fish will appreciate dark fine substrates and plenty of live plants and will bring out the brilliant colouration of the pearl gourami.

Tank mates should be peaceful, and should not be excessively large in size or overly boisterous. Pearl gouramis are at home with other community species like angelfish, tetra, barbs, danio and other similar species.

Gourimis love a mix of flakes, crisps, freeze-dried blood worms or black worms, brine shrimp and frozen foods.

Three Spot Gourami

Also known as the blue gourami, cosby gourami, gold gourami, or the opaline gourami.

Scientific Name: Trichopodus Trichopterus
Care Level: Easy
Temperament: Peaceful
Maximum Size: 6" (15cm)
Minimum Tank Size: 30 Gallons (100 litre)
Water Conditions: 72-82° F, 22-27° C, KH 2-25, pH 6.0-7.5
Diet: Omnivore
Aquarium Type: Community

Notes:
Only house one male per aquarium, as this species has a tendency to fight with one another.

You should provide lots of hiding places such as rocks and driftwood, and leave plenty of swimming area in the centre to accommodate its lively antics. This fish is an accomplished jumper, so a tight-fitting cover is a must.

He loves tubifex worms, earthworms, glass worms and brine shrimp, as well as flake and freeze-dried foods. Supplement with spirulina-based foods or blanched vegetables, such as lettuce, courgette/zucchini or peas

Golden Gourami

Usually bright yellow/gold in colour and sometimes deep orange with light stripes along its back.

Scientific Name: Trichopodus Trichopterus Gold
Care Level: Easy
Temperament: Peaceful
Maximum Size: 6" (15cm)
Minimum Tank Size: 30 Gallons (100 litre)
Water Conditions: 74-86° F, 24-30° C, KH 5-18, pH 6.5-8.0
Diet: Omnivore
Aquarium Type: Community

Notes:
This fish will appreciate dark fine substrates and plenty of live plants and will bring out the brilliant colouration of the gold gourami.

Some remain peaceful while others can become more aggressive, sometimes attacking smaller fish. Among themselves the males are territorial and will squabble. The best tankmates are other fish that are of similar size and temperament.

Gouramis love a mix of flakes, crisps, freeze-dried blood worms or black worms, brine shrimp and frozen foods.

Pygmy Sparkling Gourami

This fish sparkles with red, green, and blue colours, and can produce an audible croaking noise using a specialised pectoral mechanism.

Scientific Name: Trichopsis Vittata
Care Level: Easy
Temperament: Peaceful
Maximum Size: 1 ½" (4cm)
Minimum Tank Size: 10 Gallons (40 litre)
Water Conditions: 72-78° F, 22-25° C, KH 4-8, pH 6.0-7.0
Diet: Omnivore
Origin: Cambodia
Aquarium Type: Community

Notes:
This fish will thrive in an aquarium with live plants and rocks or driftwood amongst which it can, dark substrate brings out the best colouration of the sparkling gourami.

He can be kept with a variety of tank mates of similar size and temperament.

Gouramis love a mix of flakes, crisps, freeze-dried blood worms or black worms, brine shrimp and frozen foods.

Silver/Moonlight Gourami

This gourami is silvery coloured with a slightly greenish hue similar to the soft glow of moonlight.

Scientific Name: Trichopodus Microlepis
Care Level: Easy
Temperament: Peaceful
Maximum Size: 6" (15cm)
Minimum Tank Size: 30 Gallons (100 litre)
Water Conditions: 77-86° F, 25-30° C, KH 2-25, pH 6.0-7.5
Diet: Omnivore
Origin: Thailand
Aquarium Type: Community

Notes:
This fish will appreciate dark fine substrates and plenty of live plants and will bring out the brilliant colouration

Do not keep with fish small enough to fit in its mouth such as neons, small tetras or shrimps. Ideal tankmates include other Trichogaster, colisa, botia, corydoras, barbs, angelfish and loricariids. Males may become territorial with other males and gouramis.

These guys are omnivores and will eat a variety of foods including flake food, frozen brine shrimp, algae flakes and bloodworms.

Kissing Gourami

This fish will appreciate dark fine substrates and plenty of plants and will bring out the brilliant colouration.

Scientific Name: Helostoma Temminckii (Helostomatidae Family)
Care Level: Moderate
Temperament: Semi-aggressive
Maximum Size: 6" (15cm)
Minimum Tank Size: 30 Gallons (100 litre)
Water Conditions: 72-84° F, 22-28° C, KH 5-20, pH 6.0-8.0
Diet: Omnivore
Origin: Southeast Asia
Aquarium Type: Community

Notes:
These fish also like nibbling on live plants so if you intend of having plants, use either plastic or very hardy live plants. They're quite entertaining when they start their kissing action whether that's on each-other, the aquarium floor or decor.

Kissing gourami do well with peaceful to semi-aggressive tank mates, but may eat very small fish like neon tetras or similar small fish species.

Gourimis love a mix of flakes, crisps, freeze-dried blood worms or black worms, brine shrimp and frozen foods.

Siamese "Betta" Fighting Fish

The betta fish are know for their known for their brilliant colours and large, flowing fins of green, brown, red and grey.

Scientific Name: Betta Splendens
Care Level: Easy
Temperament: Peaceful but only 1 male must be kept per tank
Maximum Size: 3" (7cm)
Minimum Tank Size: 10 Gallons (40 litre)
Water Conditions: 75-86° F, 23-30° C, KH 0-20, pH 6.0-8.0
Diet: Carnivore
Origin: Thailand
Aquarium Type: Community

Notes:
Only one male should be kept in an aquarium as two males will fight to the death. However, females may be housed together with caution.

These guys should be housed with fish that will not nip at the betta's large fins. So no barbs.

Betta prefers a tank with a variety of hiding places amongst the foliage of freshwater plants.

Feed your betta a carnivore diet consisting of a quality flake food, frozen or freeze dried bloodworms and brine shrimp.

Cyprinids

Cyprinids belong to the Cyprinidae family. They make great fish for the beginner fish keeper as they are undemanding and easy to care for. They do well in most water conditions, though they usually prefer soft, slightly acidic water.

They do like their environment kept clean, so will need regular partial water changes.

The aquarium temperatures they require are consistent with what is needed for most tropical fish, with a range around 75° F (24°C).

If kept in a school they will usually swim out in the open. They form quite a spectacular display if you have 20 or more in a tank.

Bright lighting and distractions outside of the tank will not be a big concern, unless it is feeding time, and then they will be excited!

Black Ruby Barb

This fish is a dark ruby red in colour and usually has black fins and darker in colour towards the tail.

Scientific Name: Pethia Nigrofasciatus
Care Level: Easy
Temperament: Peaceful
Maximum Size: 2.5" (6cm)
Minimum Tank Size: 30 Gallons (100 litre)
Water Conditions: 68-79° F, 20-26° C, KH 8-12, pH 5.5-7.5
Diet: Omnivore
Origin: Indonesia
Aquarium Type: Community

Notes:
These fish are peaceful but should not be kept with long finned fish such as guppies and bettas. They must be kept in groups of 5 or more.

The aquarium should be set up with dark décor and plenty of plants in order to form much appreciated shady hiding areas. They will, however, nibble on fine-leaved plants.

Feed them flake, green flake, spinach, small frozen foods such as daphnia.

Checker Barb

This barb can be identified by its distinctive black and silver/green checked markings along the side of its body.

Scientific Name: Oliotus Oligolepis
Care Level: Easy
Temperament: Peaceful
Maximum Size: 2" (5cm)
Minimum Tank Size: 30 Gallons (100 litre)
Water Conditions: 68-79° F, 20-26° C, KH 8-12, pH 5.5-7.5
Diet: Omnivore
Origin: Indonesia
Aquarium Type: Community

Notes:
These fish are peaceful but should not be kept with long finned fish such as guppies and bettas. They must be kept in groups of 5 or more.

The aquarium should be set up with dark décor and plenty of plants in order to form much appreciated shady hiding areas.

Feed them flake, green flake, spinach, small frozen foods such as daphnia.

Cherry Barb

These little barbs are bright red in colour and usually have a dotted black pattern along the sides.

Scientific Name: Puntius Titteya
Care Level: Easy
Temperament: Peaceful
Maximum Size: 2" (5cm)
Minimum Tank Size: 30 Gallons (100 litre)
Water Conditions: 74-80° F, 23-26° C, KH 4-18, pH 6.0-7.5
Diet: Omnivore
Origin: Sri Lanka
Aquarium Type: Community

Notes:
These fish are peaceful but should not be kept with long finned fish such as guppies and bettas. They must be kept in groups of 5 or more.

The aquarium should be set up with dark décor and plenty of plants in order to form much appreciated shady hiding areas.

Feed them flake, green flake, spinach, small frozen foods such as daphnia.

Clown Barb

The clown barb is usually silver in colour with black horizontal check marks along the sides of the body.

Scientific Name: Barbodes Everetti
Care Level: Easy
Temperament: Peaceful
Maximum Size: 6" (15cm)
Minimum Tank Size: 55 Gallons (200 litre)
Water Conditions: 75-85° F, 23-29° C, KH 2-10, pH 6.0-7.0
Diet: Omnivore
Origin: Southeast Asia, Malaysia, Indonesia
Aquarium Type: Community

Notes:
These fish are an active species and should be housed in aquaria 4ft long. Keep in shoals of 5 or more fish with similar sized tank mates. They make great companions for some medium sized loaches.

These barbs will eat soft-leaved plants but should be kept in tanks with dark décor and plenty of robust plants in order to form much appreciated shady hiding areas.

Feed them flake, green flake, slow-sinking pellet foods, lettuce, spinach, frozen foods.

Flying Fox

This fish usually has an olive brown colouring on its belly with a dark black line and a gold streak from its mouth/eye to tail.

Scientific Name: Epalzeorhynchos Kalopterus
Care Level: Easy
Temperament: Peaceful
Maximum Size: 5" (12cm)
Minimum Tank Size: 55 Gallons (200 litre)
Water Conditions: 73-81° F, 22-27° C, KH 2-12, pH 6.0-7.5
Diet: Omnivore
Origin: Indonesia
Aquarium Type: Community

Notes:
These fish should be kept in groups of 5 or more and are compatible with angelfish, barbs, danios, gouramis, knifefish, loaches, tetras and rasboras. Sometimes the Flying Fox be a little aggressive towards other smaller aquarium fish if it is hungry, resulting in eating them.

Give them an aquarium with plenty of broad-leaved plants, rocks, and driftwood to serve as hiding places

Feed them flakes, wafers and tablets, vegetables such as spinach, zucchini and lettuce.

Golden Barb

This barb has greenish/yellow markings on its sides with light reddish brown colouring on its back.

Scientific Name: Barbodes Semifasciolatus
Care Level: Easy
Temperament: Peaceful
Maximum Size: 3" (7cm)
Minimum Tank Size: 20 Gallons (70 litre)
Water Conditions: 74-84° F, 23-28° C, KH 5-20, pH 6.0-7.5
Diet: Omnivore
Origin: Southeast Asia
Aquarium Type: Community

Notes:
These fish are peaceful but should not be kept with long finned fish such as guppies and bettas. They must be kept in groups of 5 or more.

The aquarium should be set up with dark décor and plenty of plants in order to form much appreciated shady hiding areas. They will, however, nibble on fine-leaved plants.

Feed them a good quality flake, green flake, spinach, small frozen foods such as daphnia.

Odessa Barb & One-spot Barb

This fish usually has bright red colouring on its sides with a beige to light brown body.

Scientific Name: Pethia Padamya
Care Level: Easy
Temperament: Peaceful
Maximum Size: 3" (7cm)
Minimum Tank Size: 20 Gallons (70 litre)
Water Conditions: 72-82° F, 22-27° C, KH 6-16, pH 6.0-7.5
Diet: Omnivore
Origin: Southeast Asia
Aquarium Type: Community

Notes:
These fish are peaceful but should not be kept with long finned fish such as guppies and bettas. They must be kept in groups of 5 or more.

The aquarium should be set up with dark décor and plenty of plants in order to form much appreciated shady hiding areas. They will, however, nibble on fine-leaved plants.

Feed them a flake, green flake, spinach, small frozen foods such as daphnia.

Red Line Torpedo Barb

This fish has silver scales with a torpedo shaped body and a distinctive black stripe running along its side with red markings over the eye.

Scientific Name: Sahyadria Denisonii
Care Level: Easy
Temperament: Peaceful
Maximum Size: 6" (15cm)
Minimum Tank Size: 55 Gallons (200 litre)
Water Conditions: 64-77° F, 17-25° C, KH 2-10, pH 6.0-7.0
Diet: Omnivore
Origin: India
Aquarium Type: Specialist Community

Notes:
These fish are an active species and should be housed in aquaria 4ft long. Keep in shoals of 5 or more fish with similar sized tank mates. They make great companions for other medium sized fish such as the loach and rainbowfish species, other barbs or larger danios.

These barbs will eat soft-leaved plants but should be kept in tanks with dark décor and plenty of robust plants in order to form much appreciated shady hiding areas.

Feed them flake, green flake, slow-sinking pellet foods, lettuce, spinach, frozen foods.

Tiger Barb

These barbs are usually silver/light brown with dark vertical black strips along the side of its body.

Scientific Name: Puntigrus Tetrazona
Care Level: Easy
Temperament: Peaceful
Maximum Size: 3" (7cm)
Minimum Tank Size: 20 Gallons (70 litre)
Water Conditions: 70-79° F, 21-26° C, KH 6-20, pH 6.0-8.0
Diet: Omnivore
Origin: Southeast Asia
Aquarium Type: Community

Notes:
These fish are peaceful but should not be kept with long finned fish such as guppies and bettas. They must be kept in groups of 8 or more.

The aquarium should be set up with dark décor and plenty of plants in order to form much appreciated shady hiding areas.

Feed them a good quality flake, green flake, micropellets, slow-sinking pellets (for larger specimens) and frozen foods.

Tinfoil Barb

Tinfoil barbs are bright silver in colour with red markings on the tail and pectoral fins

Scientific Name: Barbonymus Schwanenfeldii
Care Level: Easy
Temperament: Peaceful
Maximum Size: 12" (30cm)
Minimum Tank Size: 70 Gallons (250 litre)
Water Conditions: 72-82° F, 22-27° C, KH 6-20, pH 6.0-8.0
Diet: Omnivore
Origin: Indonesia
Aquarium Type: Community

Notes:
These fish are peaceful and mix well with other medium-large sized fish of similar temperament are more than capable of eating small fish.

The aquarium must be covered with a sturdy hood as these fish can jump, and an adult fish can be pretty weighty. They must be kept in groups of 6 or more in an aquarium with dark décor and plenty of plants in order to form much appreciated shady hiding areas. Plants should be robust as this fish will eat aquatic plants.

Feed them flake, small sinking pellets, or small frozen foods such as mosquito larvae, brineshrimp and daphnia. The larger fish will enjoy bigger frozen foods such as krill, Mysis shrimp, and chopped prawns/cockle.

Bala Shark

Also known as the shark minnow and have a silver body with black markings on the fins.

Scientific Name: Balantiocheilos Melanopterus
Care Level: Moderate
Temperament: Peaceful
Maximum Size: 12" (30cm)
Minimum Tank Size: 90 Gallons (400 litre)
Water Conditions: 72-82° F, 22-27° C, KH 6-20, pH 6.0-8.0
Diet: Omnivore
Origin: Indonesia
Aquarium Type: Specialist Community

Notes:
This fish should be kept in groups of 6 or and is only recommended for large aquariums. Tanks should be planted at the sides and back, leaving a large open swimming area in the centre. These fish should not be housed with any aggressive species.

Décor must be chosen with care as anything sharp can cause them injury whenever they decide to make a dash for cover.

Feed them a varied diet of flake, slow-sinking pellets, frozen foods such as mosquito larvae, brineshrimp, Mysis shrimp. Larger specimens will eat krill.

Red-Tailed Black Shark

The red tailed shark is jet black in colour with a brightly coloured red tail

Scientific Name: Epalzeorhynchos Bicolor
Care Level: Moderate
Temperament: Peaceful but more aggressive with age
Maximum Size: 6" (15cm)
Minimum Tank Size: 70 Gallons (250 litre)
Water Conditions: 72-82° F, 22-27° C, KH 6-20, pH 6.0-8.0
Diet: Omnivore
Origin: Thailand
Aquarium Type: Specialist Community

Notes:
These sharks are very territorial, and should be kept as a single specimen with no similar species.

The aquarium should be at least 4ft long and should have a fine substrate in order to protect the delicate sensory barbel area. Hiding places amongst rocky caves, bogwood and live plants will be very much appreciated. This fish mixes well with medium sized barbs, danios, rainbow fish and larger species of tetra, etc, that occupy a higher level in the tank.

Feed him sinking catfish pellets, flake, green flake, algae wafers, algae growing in the tank, vegetable matter, frozen foods such as mosquito larvae

Ruby Rainbow Shark

Very similar to the red tailed shark and is usually black in colour with red or orange fins.

Scientific Name: Epalzeorhynchos Frenatum
Care Level: Moderate
Temperament: Peaceful but more aggressive with age
Maximum Size: 6" (15cm)
Minimum Tank Size: 70 Gallons (250 litre)
Water Conditions: 75-82° F, 23-27° C, KH 6-18, pH 6.0-7.5
Diet: Omnivore
Origin: Thailand
Aquarium Type: Community

Notes:
These sharks are very territorial, and should be kept as a single specimen with no similar species.

The aquarium should be at least 4ft long and should have a fine substrate in order to protect the delicate sensory barbel area. Hiding places amongst rocky caves, bogwood and live plants will be very much appreciated. This fish mixes well with medium sized barbs, danios, rainbow fish and larger species of tetra, etc, that occupy a higher level in the tank.

Feed them sinking catfish pellets, flake, green flake, algae wafers, algae growing in the tank, vegetable matter, frozen foods such as mosquito larvae

Siamese Algae Eater

This algae eater is usually silver in colour with a long black stripe across the centre of its body.

Scientific Name: Crossocheilus Oblongus
Care Level: Easy
Temperament: Peaceful
Maximum Size: 6" (15cm)
Minimum Tank Size: 40 Gallons (150 litre)
Water Conditions: 75-82° F, 23-27° C, KH 6-18, pH 5.5-7.5
Diet: Herbivore
Origin: Thailand
Aquarium Type: Community

Notes:
These fish make great companions for barbs, rasboras, loaches, rainbowfish, and some of the larger tetra species. However, it is best to avoid close relatives/similar looking species.

A tank with hiding places amongst rocky caves, bogwood and live plants will be appreciated.

Feed them a diet of sinking catfish pellets, algae wafers, small frozen foods, cucumber, spinach etc. They will browses the tank surfaces for several different types of algae.

Harlequin Rasbora

This fish usually is usually orange red with a black marking towards the back of its body much resembling a pork chop shape.

Scientific Name: Trigonostigma Heteromorpha
Care Level: Easy
Temperament: Peaceful
Maximum Size: 2" (5cm)
Minimum Tank Size: 40 Gallons (150 litre)
Water Conditions: 75-82° F, 22-27° C, KH 6-12, pH 5.0-7.0
Diet: Herbivore
Origin: Thailand
Aquarium Type: Community

Notes:
Affectionately known as "pork chop" these fish make a spectacular display when kept in groups of 10 or more and seem compatible with most other fish not big enough to eat it.

A tank with hiding places amongst rocky caves, bogwood and live plants will be appreciated.

Feed them a diet of flakes, micro pellets, small frozen foods such as mosquito larvae, brineshrimp and daphnia.

Danios

Danios belong to the Cyprinidae family come are from the fresh water streams of Southeast Asia.

They are usually pretty hardy and can tolerate a wide range of tank conditions, making them perfect for beginners.

Many species are brightly coloured, and are active schooling fish. They can make spectacular displays when kept in large groups.

Giant Danio

This danio has blue and yellow markings along the side of its body with greyish clear fins.

Scientific Name: Devario Aequipinnatus
Care Level: Easy
Temperament: Semi-Aggressive
Maximum Size: 4" (10cm)
Minimum Tank Size: 10 Gallons (40 litre)
Water Conditions: 64-78° F, 17-25° C, KH 8-12, pH 6.0-7.8
Diet: Omnivore
Origin: Sri-lanka
Aquarium Type: Specialist Community

Notes:
Danios appreciate the presence of plants, driftwood, rocks and other similar decor in order to give them someplace to retreat.

Tank mates should include other semi-aggressive fish species and this fish may bully other species. These danios shoal in nature, so should be kept in groups of 8 or more.

Feed them flake foods, freeze-dried foods, blood worms, tubifex worms, brine shrimp along with some frozen foods.

Pearl Danio

This danio usually has brownish/yellow, pink/silver body and two
light yellow/white or blue/red stripes along its side.

Scientific Name: Danio Albolineatus
Care Level: Easy
Temperament: Peaceful
Maximum Size: 2.5" (6cm)
Minimum Tank Size: 10 Gallons (40 litre)
Water Conditions: 64-78° F, 17-25° C, KH 8-12, pH 6.0-7.8
Diet: Omnivore
Origin: Pakistan
Aquarium Type: Community

Notes:
Danios appreciate the presence of plants, driftwood, rocks and other
similar decor in order to give them someplace to retreat.

Tank mates should include other peaceful to semi-aggressive fish
species that are not large enough to eat danios. These fish shoal in
nature, so should be kept in groups of 8 or more.

Feed them flake foods, freeze-dried foods, blood worms, tubifex worms,
brine shrimp along with some frozen foods.

Glowlight Danio

This fish has orange bands and a series of vertical blue-black bars along its sides.

Scientific Name: Danio Choprai
Care Level: Easy
Temperament: Peaceful
Maximum Size: 1.2" (4cm)
Minimum Tank Size: 20 Gallons (80 litre)
Water Conditions: 72-79°F, 22-26° C, KH 2-10, pH 6.0-7.0
Diet: Omnivore
Origin: Myanmar
Aquarium Type: Community

Notes:
Danios appreciate the presence of plants, driftwood, rocks and other similar decor in order to give them someplace to retreat. Plus a tank with a good lid as they are good jumpers

Tank mates should include other peaceful fish species that are not large enough to eat danios. These fish shoal in nature, so should be kept in groups of 8 or more.

Feed them flake foods, freeze-dried foods, blood worms, tubifex worms, brine shrimp along with some frozen foods.

Zebra Danio

This fish has a series of blue and silver/gold stripes along the side of the body.

Scientific Name: Danio Choprai
Care Level: Easy
Temperament: Peaceful
Maximum Size: 3" (7cm)
Minimum Tank Size: 10 Gallons (40 litre)
Water Conditions: 64-78° F, 17-25° C, KH 8-12, pH 6.0-7.8
Diet: Omnivore
Origin: Pakistan
Aquarium Type: Community

Notes:
Danios appreciate the presence of plants, driftwood, rocks and other similar decor in order to give them someplace to retreat.

Tank mates should include other peaceful to semi-aggressive fish species that are not large enough to eat zebra danios. These fish shoal in nature, so should be kept in groups of 10 or more.

Feed them flake foods, freeze-dried foods, blood worms, tubifex worms, brine shrimp along with some frozen foods.

Glofish Danio

Glofish danios are genetically enhanced for their colour and come in neon red, orange, blue, green, and purple. These fish are not dyed.

Scientific Name: Danio Rerio
Care Level: Easy
Temperament: Peaceful
Maximum Size: 3" (7cm)
Minimum Tank Size: 10 Gallons (40 litre)
Water Conditions: 64-78° F, 17-25° C, KH 8-12, pH 6.5-7.5
Diet: Omnivore
Origin: Captive-bred
Aquarium Type: Community

Notes:
These fish are a luminous colour and glow when the aquarium lights come on. They make a spectacular display when stocked in groups of 15 or more.

Tank mates should include other peaceful to semi-aggressive fish species that are not large enough to eat danios.

Feed them flake foods, freeze-dried foods, blood worms, tubifex worms, brine shrimp along with some frozen foods.

Chapter 11

Angels & Cichlids

Cichlids, pronounced "sick-lid", belong to the Cichlidae family. There are over a thousand species of cichlid, the majority of which originate from the Malawi, Tanganyika & Victoria rift lakes in Central Africa. Cichlids are known for their striking colourations, interesting behaviours and extroverted personalities.

African cichlids are quite aggressive and territorial, but given the right aquarium setup and mixture of species, they can coexist and thrive within the aquarium environment.

New World Cichlids or South American Cichlids are quite hardy and come from parts of the Amazon River.

The Angelfish is a very popular cichlid from the Amazon basin. Angels can grow to about six inches long and a height of eight inches. The distinctive shape of the body and fins adds variety to the community aquarium. The tank should be deep enough for the Angelfish to swim comfortably with its fins extended.

Altum Angelfish

This angel is silver with three brownish/red vertical stripes and red and black markings on the dorsal fin.

Scientific Name: Pterophyllum Altum
Care Level: Moderate
Temperament: Semi-aggressive
Maximum Size: 6" (15cm)
Minimum Tank Size: 55 Gallons (200 litre)
Water Conditions: 75-82° F, 13-27° C, KH 1-5, pH 5.8-6.5
Diet: Omnivore
Origin: Amazon
Aquarium Type: Community

Notes:
Angels love tanks with plenty of plants and driftwood. A group freshwater Angelfish are territorial and will squabble with one another until a dominant male is established.

They can be kept singularly, in mated pairs or in medium sized groups of 6 or more with other fish species that are large enough not to be eaten.

They will readily consume flake, pellet and frozen foods.

Koi Angelfish

This angel is mostly white with black markings and bright orange on its head.

Scientific Name: Pterophyllum Scalare
Care Level: Moderate
Temperament: Semi-aggressive
Maximum Size: 6" (15cm)
Minimum Tank Size: 55 Gallons (200 litre)
Water Conditions: 75-82° F, 23-27° C, KH 1-5, pH 6.0-7.0
Diet: Omnivore
Origin: Amazon
Aquarium Type: Community

Notes:
Angels love tanks with plenty of plants and driftwood. A group freshwater Angelfish are territorial and will squabble with one another until a dominant male is established.

They can be kept singularly, in mated pairs or in medium sized groups of 6 or more with other fish species that are large enough not to be eaten.

They will readily consume flake, pellet and frozen foods.

Gold Angelfish

This angel is mostly silver with gold markings on its head and dorsal fin.

Scientific Name: Pterophyllum Scalare
Care Level: Moderate
Temperament: Semi-aggressive
Maximum Size: 6" (15cm)
Minimum Tank Size: 55 Gallons (200 litre)
Water Conditions: 75-82° F, 23-27° C, KH 1-5, pH 6.0-7.0
Diet: Omnivore
Origin: Amazon
Aquarium Type: Community

Notes:
Angels love tanks with plenty of plants and driftwood. A group freshwater Angelfish are territorial and will squabble with one another until a dominant male is established.

They can be kept singularly, in mated pairs or in medium sized groups of 6 or more with other fish species that are large enough not to be eaten.

They will readily consume flake, pellet and frozen foods.

Green Terror Cichlid

This cichlid is usually greenish white with blue spots under the mouth area.

Scientific Name: Andinoacara Rivulatus
Care Level: Moderate
Temperament: Aggressive; little monster
Maximum Size: 12" (30cm)
Minimum Tank Size: 75 Gallons (300 litre)
Water Conditions: 73-79° F, 22-26° C, KH 10-20, pH 6.5-8.0
Diet: Omnivore
Origin: South America
Aquarium Type: Cichlid-American

Notes:
Keep with fish of mild temperament and other cichlid species and are very aggressive towards other peaceful species.

Feed them a variety of foods including cichlid pellets, flakes, bloodworms, and shrimp

Oscar

Oscars are very popular, have distinct personalities and can be quite entertaining and playful.

Scientific Name: Astronnotus Ocellatus
Care Level: Moderate
Temperament: Peaceful
Maximum Size: 12" (30cm)
Minimum Tank Size: 75 Gallons (300 litre)
Water Conditions: 73-79° F, 22-26° C, KH 5-20, pH 6.5-8.0
Diet: Carnivore
Origin: South America
Aquarium Type: Cichlid-American

Notes:
Don't keep this fish with fish small enough to fit in his mouth and should be kept with similar sized fish.

Oscars like to re-arrange the tank, so make sure any rocks and decor you add don't have sharp edges and that filters and heaters are securely attached and guarded. Give them some sand or gravel on the floor of the tank.

Give them meaty foods and are fond of earth worms. Treat them to insects such as live crickets which are available from any pet store.

Rams

These fish are gold, yellow, blue, and black with a red patch on the abdomen.

Scientific Name: Mikrogeophagus Ramirezi
Care Level: Expert
Temperament: Peaceful
Maximum Size: 3" (7cm)
Minimum Tank Size: 20 Gallons (80 litre)
Water Conditions: 72-80° F, 22-26° C, KH 5-10, pH 5.0-7.0
Diet: Omnivore
Origin: South America
Aquarium Type: Cichlid-American

Notes:
Rams are best housed in groups of 5 or more individuals. While they are peaceful towards other tank mates, they fight amongst themselves to establish a group hierarchy.

They prefer aquariums with a sand, gravel or mixed substrate, plenty of plants and driftwood.

Feed them meaty flakes, mini-pellets, freeze-dried worms and frozen brine and shrimp..

Convict Cichlid

This cichlid has an elongated shape with black and white vertical stripes across its body.

Scientific Name: Archocentrus Nigrofasciatus
Care Level: Moderate
Temperament: Territorial
Maximum Size: 6" (15cm)
Minimum Tank Size: 20 Gallons (80 litre)
Water Conditions: 68-79° F, 20-26° C, KH 10-20, pH 6.5-8.0
Diet: Omnivore
Origin: South America
Aquarium Type: Cichlid-American

Notes:
Provide a clay or plastic type of cave (flower pot).

The do best in a species only tank or with other cichlids species and should be housed with species larger or of similar size and temperament.

They should accept nearly all aquarium fish foods including flakes, frozen, freeze dried, live and cichild pellets.

Jack Dempsey Cichlid

This cichlid, named after the famous boxer, is dark brown in colour, with iridescent green and blue spots along its sides.

Scientific Name: Rocio Octofasciata
Care Level: Easy
Temperament: Aggressive
Maximum Size: 10" (25cm)
Minimum Tank Size: 55 Gallons (200 litre)
Water Conditions: 78-82° F, 23-27° C, KH 5-10, pH 6.5-8.0
Diet: Carnivore
Origin: Central America
Aquarium Type: Cichlid-American

Notes:
Keep this fish with other cichlid species and not with peaceful fish. These fish are territorial and will eat small fish.

Keep them in an aquarium with fine sand, with plenty of rocks and hiding places. Any plants should be hardy as these fish are known to dig up plants and destroy the leaves.

This fish is mostly carnivorous and will eat cichlid pellets, flakes, bloodworms, shrimp and fish small enough to fit in its mouth.

Bumblebee Cichlid

This cichlid has an elongate body with vertical yellow-and-black along the side of its body.

Scientific Name: Pseudotropheus Crabro
Care Level: Moderate
Temperament: Aggressive; bully
Maximum Size: 8" (20cm)
Minimum Tank Size: 75 Gallons (300 litre)
Water Conditions: 75-82° F, 23-27° C, KH 10-15, pH 7.5-8.5
Diet: Omnivore
Origin: Lake Malawi
Aquarium Type: Cichlid-African

Notes:
Keep with fish of mild temperament and other cichlid species. The do best in a species only tank or with other cichlids from Lake Malawi.

These guys do best in a cichlid community tank with other african cichlids and should not be kept with peaceful fish.

Feed them a variety of foods including cichlid pellets, flakes, bloodworms, and shrimp. Get them on a good pellet food made for cichlids (cichlid sticks)

Blue Dolphin Cichlid

This cichlid has an elongated shape with a cranial hump, striking dark and light blues along the side of its body.

Scientific Name: Cyrtocara Moorii
Care Level: Moderate
Temperament: Semi-Aggressive
Maximum Size: 10" (25cm)
Minimum Tank Size: 75 Gallons (300 litre)
Water Conditions: 75-82° F, 23-27° C, KH 10-15, pH 7.5-8.5
Diet: Omnivore
Origin: Lake Malawi
Aquarium Type: Cichlid-African

Notes:
These fish do best in a species only tank or with other cichlids from Lake Malawi.

This fish is best kept with fish of the same size and are not suitable for community tanks

Feed them a variety of foods including cichlid pellets, flakes, bloodworms, and shrimp. Get them on a good pellet food made for cichlids (cichlid sticks)

Kribensis Cichlid

This cichlid has an elongated shape with black and yellow stripes on the side of its body, with a fiery red belly.

Scientific Name: Pelvicachromis pulcher
Care Level: Easy
Temperament: Semi-Aggressive
Maximum Size: 4" (10cm)
Minimum Tank Size: 55 Gallons (200 litre)
Water Conditions: 72-82° F, 22-27° C, KH 5-10, pH 6.5-8.5
Diet: Omnivore
Origin: Nigeria
Aquarium Type: Cichlid-African

Notes:
Provide them with plenty of rocks and caves with a sandy substrate as they love to borrow

These guys can be territorial, so use caution when adding them to community aquariums and will nip fins of betta, guppies and angels.

Feed them a variety of foods including cichlid pellets and bloodworms. Get them on a good pellet food made for cichlids (cichlid sticks)

Discus

Discus Fish belong to the Cichlidae family and are the native of the Amazon River.

They are very shy and docile fish, which are best kept with their own species in an aquarium tank.

They can be a bit expensive and get quite big, but in a large aquarium they can make an impressive display with their bright colours and slow graceful moving character.

These fish usually require an advanced level of care due to its feeding requirements and water filtration. They require pristine water conditions, soft, slightly acidic water, with plenty of water changes to control the toxins (about 25% of the tank a week).

Common Discus

Known for its disc shaped body these fish are brightly coloured and are frequently patterned in shades of green, red, brown, and blue.

Scientific Name: Symphysodon Aequifasciatus
Care Level: Moderate
Temperament: Peaceful
Maximum Size: 8" (20cm)
Minimum Tank Size: 55 Gallons (200 litre)
Water Conditions: 78-86° F, 25-30° C, KH 1-3, pH 6.0-7.5
Diet: Omnivore
Origin: Amazon, South America
Aquarium Type: Community

Notes:
These fish require very consistent water parameters that have very little pH, temperature and does not leave a lot of room for error.

They appreciate a tank with plenty of live plants, cover, rocks, etc and can be housed with most tetra species, loaches, cory catfish, smaller plecos, siamese algae eaters, peaceful rasbora species, Rainbow fish, Hatchet fish and pencilfish.

Feed them a variety of nutritional meaty foods including: white worms, blood worms, Tubifex worms, and high protein pellet or flake foods.

133

Royal Red Discus

Known for its disc shaped body these fish are brightly coloured with a beautiful shade of red, and black markings on their tail fin.

Scientific Name: Symphysodon Aequifasciatus
Care Level: Moderate
Temperament: Peaceful
Maximum Size: 8" (20cm)
Minimum Tank Size: 55 Gallons (200 litre)
Water Conditions: 79-86° F, 25-30° C, KH 1-3, pH 6.0-7.5
Diet: Omnivore
Origin: Amazon, South America
Aquarium Type: Community

Notes
They appreciate a tank with plenty of live plants, cover, rocks, etc and can be housed with most tetra species, loaches, cory catfish, smaller plecos, siamese algae eaters, peaceful rasbora species, Rainbow fish, Hatchet fish and pencilfish.

Feed him freeze-dried bloodworms and tubifex, Discus pellets, high-quality flake food, and meaty frozen foods.

Red Checkerboard Discus

This discus fish is brightly coloured with a beautiful white, red and orange markings.

Scientific Name: Symphysodon Aequifasciatus
Care Level: Moderate
Temperament: Peaceful
Maximum Size: 8" (20cm)
Minimum Tank Size: 55 Gallons (200 litre)
Water Conditions: 79-86° F, 25-30° C, KH 1-3, pH 6.0-7.5
Diet: Omnivore
Origin: Amazon, South America
Aquarium Type: Community

Notes
They appreciate a tank with plenty of live plants, cover, rocks, etc and can be housed with most tetra species, loaches, cory catfish, smaller plecos, siamese algae eaters, peaceful rasbora species, Rainbow fish, Hatchet fish and pencilfish.

Feed him freeze-dried bloodworms and tubifex, Discus pellets, high-quality flake food, and meaty frozen foods.

Rainbow Fish

The rainbowfish belong to the Melanotaeniidae family and are colourful, freshwater fish found in Australia, New Guinea, islands in Cenderawasih Bay, and the Raja Ampat Islands.

Red Rainbowfish

These fish are bright red in colour, with sections of orange colouring on its head and back.

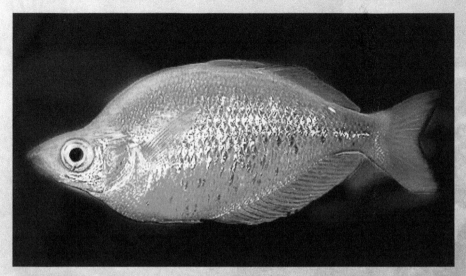

Scientific Name: Glossolepis Incisus
Care Level: Easy
Temperament: Peaceful
Maximum Size: 5" (12cm)
Minimum Tank Size: 55 Gallons (200 litre)
Water Conditions: 75-82° F, 23-27° C, KH 9-19, pH 7.0-8.0
Diet: Omnivore
Origin: Southeast Asia, New Guinea
Aquarium Type: Community

Notes:
Provide them with a long aquarium that has plenty plants and room for these active swimmers to move about. They are also well known jumpers so the aquarium should be well covered. These fish are schooling fish and should be kept in groups of 6 or more individuals

Feed them flake, frozen and freeze-dried fish foods fed 2 to 3 times per day is ideal.

Boeseman's Rainbowfish

This fish has fiery red with orange and yellow highlights along its tail fin and back, going into a deep indigo blue or purple toward the front.

Scientific Name: Melanotaenia Boesemani
Care Level: Easy
Temperament: Peaceful
Maximum Size: 4" (10cm)
Minimum Tank Size: 40 Gallons (150 litre)
Water Conditions: 72-79° F, 22-26° C, KH 9-19, pH 7.0-8.0
Diet: Omnivore
Origin: Southeast Asia, Thailand
Aquarium Type: Community

Notes:
Provide them with a long aquarium that has plenty plants and room for these active swimmers to move about.

They are also well known jumpers so the aquarium should be well covered.

These fish are schooling fish and should be kept in groups of 6 or more individuals and seem compatible with most other peaceful species.

Feed them flake, frozen and freeze-dried fish foods fed 2 to 3 times per day is ideal.

Neon Rainbowfish

Also known as the dwarf rainbow fish and is bright blue with marks of red on their fins.

Scientific Name: Melanotaenia Praecox
Care Level: Easy
Temperament: Peaceful
Maximum Size: 2.5" (6cm)
Minimum Tank Size: 30 Gallons (100 litre)
Water Conditions: 70-78° F, 21-25° C, KH 8-12, pH 5.8-6.5
Diet: Omnivore
Origin: Indonesia
Aquarium Type: Community

Notes:
Provide them with a long aquarium that has plenty plants and room for these active swimmers to move about. These fish are schooling fish and should be kept in groups of 6 or more individuals

Feed them flake, frozen and freeze-dried fish foods fed 2 to 3 times per day is ideal.

Chapter 14

Neotropical Electric Fish

The black ghost knifefish is a weakly electric fish, the black ghost knifefish can both produce and sense electrical impulses.

Black Ghost Knifefish

The fish has a jet black body with two white rings on its tail, and a white blaze on its nose and head.

Scientific Name: Apteronotus albifrons
Temperament: Semi-aggressive
Maximum Size: 12" - 16" (40cm)
Minimum Tank Size: 150 Gallons (500 litre)
Water Conditions: 73-80° F, 22-26° C, KH 0-10, pH 6.5-7.0
Diet: Carnivore
Origin: South America
Family: Apteronotidae
Aquarium Type: Community

Notes:
Provide them with a long aquarium that has plenty plants and room for these swimmers to move about. They need fine gravel and a tank with subdued lighting.

These fish can be shy and timid at first but with a bit of time they can become very tame. They are peaceful with larger tank mates that are big enough to not be considered food.

He will eat all types of live foods including meat, chopped earthworms, as well as frozen, flaked foods and small fish.

Elephant Nose

This fish is dark black in colour with a long 'trunk-like' nose, forked tail with a white stripe.

Scientific Name: Gnathonemus Petersii
Care Level: Difficult
Temperament: Semi-aggressive
Maximum Size: 9" (25cm)
Minimum Tank Size: 55 Gallons (200 litre)
Water Conditions: 73-80° F, 22-27° C, KH 0-10, pH 6.5-7.0
Diet: Carnivore
Origin: Africa
Family: Mormyridae
Aquarium Type: Community

Notes:
These fish are peaceful, but cannot be kept in pairs because the weaker one will be harassed. They are compatible with any peaceful fish such as tetras, angels or gouramis.

These fish like to jump so make sure your tank has a lid. They subdued light, and places to hide.

They love brine shrimp and bloodworms, frozen or live, but will rarely accept flakes.

Chapter 15

Miscellaneous Fish

Some other common fish are in this section that are readily available in most aquariums.

Here are some of the more interesting specimens to keep.

Common Hatchet Fish

Hatchets are usually a marble colour ranging from silver and black to a more plane silver colour.

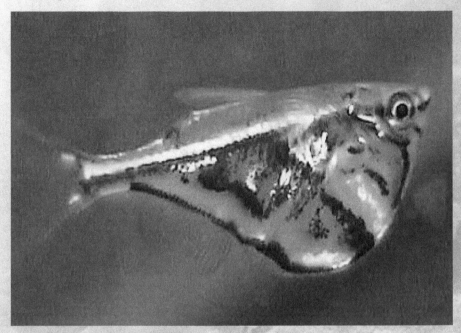

Scientific Name: Carnegiella Strigata
Temperament: Peaceful
Maximum Size: 1.5" (4cm)
Minimum Tank Size: 20 Gallons (80 litre)
Water Conditions: 73-80° F, 22-26° C, KH 2-4, pH 6.5-7.0
Diet: Carnivore
Origin: Venezuela
Family: Gasteropelecidae
Aquarium Type: Community

Notes:
These fish appreciate floating plants and prefer to be in groups of about 5 or more. Also add driftwood, fine gravel and plenty of hiding places and plant cover. Make sure you have a tight fitting cover, as these fish can jump.

These guys can be reluctant to take dried foods initially, but it will usually learn to accept them over time. Also feed them frozen and live foods, such as bloodworm or daphnia. Try a few drosophila fruit flies if you can find them.

145

Three-lined Pencil Fish

This fish usually has has three black horizontal stripes that run the length of the body.

Scientific Name: Nannostomus Trifasciatus
Temperament: Peaceful
Maximum Size: 3" (7cm)
Minimum Tank Size: 55 Gallons (200 litre)
Water Conditions: 75-82° F, 23-27° C, KH 2-5, pH 6.5-7.0
Diet: Carnivore
Origin: South America
Family: Lebiasinidae
Aquarium Type: Community

Notes:
These fish appreciate floating plants and prefer to be in groups of about 5 or more and best kept with similar sized fish. Also add driftwood, fine gravel and plenty of hiding places and plant cover.

These guys have a small mouth so you may need special food, but will accept your usual flake food. Also feed them frozen and live foods, such as bloodworm or daphnia.

Butterfly Fish

Also known as the African Butterfly Fish and is dark brown to black in colour with speckled lighter colourations.

Scientific Name: Pantodon Buchholzi
Temperament: Aggressive
Maximum Size: 5" (12cm)
Minimum Tank Size: 30 Gallons (120 litre)
Water Conditions: 75-86° F, 23-30° C, KH 1-10, pH 6.9-7.1
Diet: Carnivore
Origin: Africa
Family: Pantodontidae
Aquarium Type: Non - Community

Notes:
This fish is a predator and spends most of its time hanging at the surface of the water, waiting for prey. Keep with other aggressive fish or fish of the same size as this fish will eat fish small enough to fit in its mouth.

Set up your tank with plenty of plants that reach near the surface that this fish can use for cover. These fish can jump out of the water, and can even glide short distances so keep a tight lid on your tank

Feed him a steady diet of small fish, brine shrimp, insects and freeze-dried foods.

Panchax Killifish

This fish is vibrant blue/green or yellow with many red spots running the length of the body.

Scientific Name: Aplocheilus Lineatus
Temperament: Peaceful
Maximum Size: 2.5" (6cm)
Minimum Tank Size: 20 Gallons (80 litre)
Water Conditions: 75-86° F, 23-30° C, KH 1-10, pH 6.9-7.1
Diet: Carnivore
Origin: Sri Lanka
Family: Aplocheilidae
Aquarium Type: Community - surface dweller

Notes
There are a variety of killi fish, from golden, clown and gardneri.

The term "Killi" is derived from the Dutch word for ditch. It's not a killer or aggressive in anyway.

Feed these little guys live foods such as brine shrimp, white worms, tubifex, as well as dry flake and frozen foods. They prefer to eat from the surface of the water so any food that floats on the surface.

Parrot Cichlid

This fish is often bright red, orange, yellow or grey. Avoid the ones that have been injected with dye - this is cruel and shortens their lifespan!

Scientific Name: Hybrid Cichlid
Temperament: Peaceful
Maximum Size: 8" (20cm)
Minimum Tank Size: 30 Gallons (100 litre)
Water Conditions: 72-82° F, 22-28° C, KH 1-10, pH 6.5-7.0
Diet: Carnivore
Origin: Man-made South American cichlid hybrid
Family: Cichlid
Aquarium Type: Community - surface dweller

Notes
This fish can be quite entertaining to watch as they potter around the tank and can be housed on their own of in a group.

Feed them live foods such as brine shrimp, worms, as well as dry flake and frozen foods.

Chapter 16

Unit Conversions

The units used in this book are inches and Fahrenheit, but if you are used to the metric system in this section there is a conversion chart to enable you to convert the measurements into the system you are familiar with.

Conversion Tables

Inch	Cm	°C	°F	Litre	US Gallon
0	0.00	10	50.00	20	5.28
1	2.54	11	51.80	30	7.93
2	5.08	12	53.60	40	10.57
3	7.62	13	55.40	50	13.21
4	10.16	14	57.20	60	15.85
5	12.70	15	59.00	70	18.49
6	15.24	16	60.80	80	21.13
7	17.78	17	62.60	90	23.78
8	20.32	18	64.40	100	26.42
9	22.86	19	66.20	110	29.06
10	25.40	20	68.00	120	31.70
11	27.94	21	69.80	130	34.34
12	30.48	22	71.60	140	36.98
13	33.02	23	73.40	150	39.63
14	35.56	24	75.20	160	42.27
15	38.10	25	77.00	170	44.91
16	40.64	26	78.80	180	47.55
17	43.18	27	80.60	190	50.19
18	45.72	28	82.40	200	52.83
19	48.26	29	84.20	210	55.48
20	50.80	30	86.00	220	58.12
21	53.34	31	87.80	230	60.76
22	55.88	32	89.60	240	63.40
23	58.42	33	91.40	250	66.04
24	60.96	34	93.20	260	68.68
25	63.50	35	95.00	270	71.33
26	66.04	36	96.80	280	73.97
27	68.58	37	98.60	290	76.61
28	71.12	38	100.40	300	79.25
29	73.66	39	102.20	400	105.67
30	76.20	40	104.00	500	132.09

Index

Index

Index

CPSIA information can be obtained
at www.ICGtesting.com
Printed in the USA
LVHW05s1248110818
586672LV00006B/13/P